W9-BCR-753

MAY 1975

RECEIVED

OHIO DOMINICAN
COLLEGE LIBRARY
COLUMBUS, OHIO
43219

*TWAYNE'S WORLD AUTHORS SERIES*

*A Survey of the World's Literature*

Sylvia E. Bowman, Indiana University

GENERAL EDITOR

# INDIA

M. L. Sharma, Slippery Rock State College

EDITOR

Manohar Malgonkar

*TWAS 340*

*Photograph by Nancy Palmer, courtesy of The Viking Press*

# Manohar Malgonkar

# Manohar Malgonkar

By JAMES Y. DAYANANDA

*Lock Haven State College*

TWAYNE PUBLISHERS

A DIVISION OF G. K. HALL & CO., BOSTON

*Copyright © 1974 by Twayne Publishers, Inc.*
All Rights Reserved

Library of Congress Cataloging in Publication Data

Dayananda, James Y    1934-
  Manohar Malgonkar.

  (Twayne's world authors series, TWAS 340. India)
  Bibliography: p. 169.
  1. Malgonkar, Manohar, 1913-
PR9499.3.M3Z6        823        74-11127
ISBN 0-8057-2566-0

823.0 9
M248D

MANUFACTURED IN THE UNITED STATES OF AMERICA

For
Muddu Vanitha and Priya
in memory of shared experiences

94449

# Contents

# *About the Author*

James Yesupriya Dayananda was born in 1934. He received his B.A. (Honours) from the University of Mysore, Bangalore, India in 1956 and his Ph.D. from Temple University, Philadelphia in 1969. He has taught in the universities of Venkateshwara, Madras, and Andhra in India. His main interest is in literary criticism (history, theory and practice) and in twentieth-century literature (American and British). His articles have appeared in *Literature East and West, Journal of South Asian Literature, Lock Haven Review, Literature and Psychology, Indian Journal of American Studies,* and *World Literature Written in English.* At present he is professor of English and Chairman of the Department of English and Philosophy at Lock Haven State College, Lock Haven, Pennsylvania.

# *Preface*

Generally speaking, Indian authors in English have almost never been the subject of serious criticism. Most critics, when they have not ignored them entirely, have not gone beyond brief impressionistic reviews and patchy appreciative comments. Though certainly one of the most admired and widely read Indian novelists in English, Manohar Malgonkar has never received full critical attention as a significant contemporary novelist writing in English. This full-length study is an attempt to fill a long-standing need for an overall critical assessment of his novels. My basic aims — I believe these are the aims of all literary criticism — are to provide an exacting scrutiny of the texts and careful evaluation of their art and technique. The pages which follow trace the career of Manohar Malgonkar from the publication *Distant Drum* (1960) to *The Devil's Wind* (1972). I have chosen to review his books of history, but not his short stories and articles, because they have something significant to say about his fiction.

The design of the book is as follows:

Chapter 1 is a biographical introduction that gives facts of Malgonkar's life and publications. In this chapter through conversations in interviews, usually lively, often gay, and always penetrating, Malgonkar draws a portrait of himself.

Chapter 2 considers his growth as a novelist, surveys his novels, and discusses the continuity of major themes. The focus is on his early novels, *Distant Drum* and *Combat of Shadows,* and on the main trend of their thematic development.

Chapter 3 is entirely devoted to a discussion of Malgonkar's three books of history: *Kanhoji Angrey, Puars of Dewas Senior,* and *Chhatrapatis of Kolhapur.*

Chapter 4 looks critically at *The Princes* in which the concerns of the novelist and the historian come together. This is an attempt to apply three different critical approaches to Malgonkar's best novel to elucidate its many-faceted excellence: to see it as a document of contemporary history from the critical standpoint of historical approach, as an initiation story from the critical standpoint of the mythological approach, and as a work of complex rhythms from the critical standpoint of the formalist approach. My overall approach is not theoretical but practical and my overall hope is to produce genuine literary criticism.

Chapter 5 is a discussion of *A Bend in the Ganges* both as history and as an initiation story.

Chapter 6 is a detailed consideration of *The. Devil's Wind* as a historical novel, as at once good history and good fiction.

Chapter 7 presents some concluding observations on Malgonkar's status in the tradition of English writing outside Britain and the United States. I have drawn my impressions of Malgonkar's works together to present a careful critical estimate of his achievement.

I am deeply grateful to Mr. Malgonkar for two long interviews I had with him in September, 1972, when he spent a weekend at Lock Haven State College, Lock Haven, Pa. He impressed me as a man of great personal charm and culture. He was ready and eager to answer any question about his career and work.

This book had its origins in a course in literary criticism that I taught at Lock Haven State College in 1970. I wish to thank my students, with whom portions of this book were discussed, for their honest and stimulating reactions to Malgonkar's works.

Parts of the book were presented as papers at the Eighty-Eighth Annual Convention of the Modern Language Association on December 29, 1972, in New York at its South Asian Literature Seminar and at the Twenty-fifth Annual Meeting of the Association for Asian Studies on April 1, 1973, in Chicago at its Seminar on "Feminine Sensibility in Indian Literature." I owe thanks to the panelists at these meetings, especially to Professors Robert McDowell, editor, *World Literature Written in English* and Carlo Coppola, editor, *Journal of South Asian Literature* for providing contexts of stimulus, encouragement, and support which urged this book forward. I am also grateful to them for publishing parts of the book in their journals.

In my search for books and articles connected with the subject I was very much helped by the staff of the Stevenson Library, Lock Haven State College. I wish to thank Mr. Marc Thomas, Reference Librarian, for the readiness with which he put his expertise at my service.

## Preface

I have to thank Dr. M. Fisher for allowing me to use her unpublished interview with Malgonkar.

I owe my thanks to Mrs. Ann Peter for her competent secretarial assistance and to Miss Pramila Swamidas for her kindness in proofreading the whole book in typescript. I wish to express my gratitude to Professor Mohan Lal Sharma for his help in editing this manuscript.

JAMES Y. DAYANANDA

*Lock Haven, Pennsylvania*

# *Acknowledgments*

Grateful acknowledgment is made to the following for permission to quote from the works of Manohar Malgonkar: Asia Publishing House, New York for quotations from *Distant Drum* and *Kanhoji Angrey;* Hamish Hamilton Ltd., London, for quotations from *Combat of Shadows.* From *The Princes* by Manohar Malgonkar. Copyright © 1963 by Manohar Malgonkar. Reprinted by permission of The Viking Press, Inc. From *The Devil's Wind* by Manohar Malgonkar. Copyright © 1972 by Manohar Malgonkar. Reprinted by permission of The Viking Press, Inc. From *A Bend in the Ganges* by Manohar Malgonkar. Copyright © 1964, 1965 by Manohar Malgonkar. Reprinted by permission of The Viking Press, Inc.

# Chronology

1913  Born July 12 in Bombay.
1919-  School Years.
1931
1931-  College Years.
1935
1935  Graduated from Bombay University. B.A. (Honours) in English and Sanskrit.
1947  Marriage.
1948  Daughter, Sunita, born.
1935-  Professional Hunter.
1937
1937  Joined Central Government Service.
1942-  Years of Service in the Army. Travel in Nepal, Indonesia,
1952  Malaya, and Western Europe including England.
1952  Joined an American business firm in Delhi. Operated manganese mines.
1957  Elections in India. Unsuccessful Independent candidate for Parliament.
1959  *Kanhoji Angrey.*
1960  *Distant Drum.*
1962  Elections in India. Unsuccessful Swatantra Party Candidate for Parliament. *Combat of Shadows.*
1963  *Puars of Dewas Senior. The Princes.* First visit to the United States; lectures at Iowa, Beloit, University of Pennsylvania, and Columbia University.
1964  *A Bend in the Ganges.* Second visit to United States.
1970  Third visit to the United States; lectures at Canton, Potsdam, N.Y., American University, Washington, D.C., and Foreign Service Institute.
1971  *Chhatrapatis of Kolhapur.*

1972   *The Devil's Wind*. Fourth visit to the United States; lectures at Lock Haven State College, Gettysburg College, Washington, D.C., Manhattanville College, Purchase, N.Y. Visit to London.

# CHAPTER 1

# *Biographical Introduction*

A T seven-thirty sharp every day, Sunday included, summer or winter — in fact, just about every morning the year round — a tall broad-shouldered, twinkling-eyed, highly motivated, soft-spoken, affable, outgoing, sixty-year-old Indian writer in English sits at his desk in his study in a remote village in South India called Jagalbet, and proceeds to pound at the typewriter. He works until about 12:30 with a break of 15 minutes for breakfast. This busy, methodical man is Manohar Malgonkar, the author of five novels, three history books, and several articles and short stories. At the age of sixty Malgonkar is a trim and sprightly man with a crown of gray hair, who retains some of the bright alertness of his military career. He still continues to write, having maintained a rapid pace since 1959, when at the age of forty-six his first book, *Kanhoji Angrey,* was published. He presently has two novels with the publishers. What strikes one most about his literary career is the steady output and the evidence it gives of his determination to live by his pen. I asked him how he managed to write so much.

"Yes, that surprises me, too. What surprises me is why other people try and make out how little they can write, how creativity is such a tremendously difficult thing for them; because, you know, I wrote this whole first draft of *The Princes* in forty-nine days. Then, I left it alone and two months later I went back to it and retyped the whole thing and sent it to the publisher. And it's only since I came to America and since I started learning about the difficulty that other writers seem to experience with creativity and thought that if they wrote 500 words a day they had done a good day's work my fingers started to become diffident and I don't produce as much as I used to. . . . I started reading about writers at work and things like that about other writers when I became sufficiently and modestly established as a writer, you might say. And then I found that creativity is difficult. . . . I write sometimes as many as 4,-000 words a day."[1]

Manohar Malgonkar was born in Bombay, India, on July 12, 1913. His family comes from a jungle village — Jagalbet in Belgaum District — where they have lived for generations. They are Marathi-speaking and landowning Brahmins. Malgonkar's brother, Vibhakar, manages the family land which includes some manganese mines. Malgonkar lives in a lovely house built on this land about which John Morris writes so excitedly in his book *Eating the Indian Air* (1969).

## I  *Malgonkar's Education in English*

He went to school during 1919 - 1931 where he was taught English as a second language by Indian teachers with little or no knowledge of the living English language. These teachers spoke a brand of Indian English often unrecognizable to Englishmen themselves as their own tongue. In an article in *The Times Literary Supplement* Malgonkar writes about this aspect of his English education in detail:

English did not come naturally to us; we do not speak it in our homes. For most of us our acquaintance with the language began only after we had finished our 'primary' stage. . . . This means that in India, those of us who learn English do not come to the cat-sat-on-the-mat stage of familiarity with the language until we are well past ten years old. . . .[2]

Malgonkar learned English mainly as a written language at school and at college in Bombay University (1931 - 35). It was grammatically correct but very stiff, formal, unnatural English. The spoken language — easy, informal, natural English — Malgonkar learned not from his teachers at school and college but later in life from officials of the Empire — planters, army officers who were Englishmen, "the box wallahs and the left-overs from the British days."
He says:

The spoken English language in India, even in my college days nearly thirty years ago now . . . came to us from those who, another thirty years or so earlier had, with luck, learned it under English tutors. . . . The professor who taught me Shakespeare had never been to England, nor I think had he, except on rare occasions, used the language as a means of conversation with Englishmen themselves. He spoke an archaic, book-learned, dictionary-obsessed English in a singsong whine. . . . It is quite possible that he was entirely successful in putting across to his students the plays of Shakespeare. But did he teach us English?[3]

I asked him to describe the whole process of mastering English, mastering enough to write creatively in it. He says that his proficiency was achieved mainly through the reading of books by English, Scottish, Irish, and American writers.

"Before I started writing, I used to be a voracious reader, but then again as an average reader, you go to a library and pick half a dozen books up which you think might keep you interested, read three or four of them and study — no special interest or anything like that. Even now I read almost anything, but now I'm, after all, at an age where I have to pick and choose and I read books which will help whatever book I'm doing at the moment.

"Up to about ten years of age very few of us knew any English at all, at least I didn't. I learned to say cat-sat-on-the-mat when I was about ten years old. Afterward, I was educated formally in formal schools and I took my honors in English and Sanskrit and then I joined service under the British. You see that must affect my language, because after all I came into contact with the living English, but then as a government official of a fairly senior status my companions were mostly English, my senior officers were English. And then this stint in the Army, where all of us were English and spoke English as a natural language, . . . may have given me the background or may have given me some sort of fluency. . . . But this late exposure to the English language didn't seem to do any harm and I seemed to get a significant fluency in the language to be able to write in it after fifteen years of reading English books."

Unlike other Indian writers who were educated in the West — Mulk Raj Anand, Raja Rao, and Khushwant Singh — Malgonkar's education was totally Indian. He graduated from Bombay University in 1935 with a B.A. (Honours) in Sanskrit and English literature. Both at school and college he did not write anything — he does not remember having written anything for school or college magazines. It was only later, after trying five other careers — professional big-game hunting, civil service, army, business, and politics — that he turned to writing.

## II  *Malgonkar's Five Other Careers*

Malgonkar took to hunting at the age of ten, and from 1935 to 1937 he earned his living as a professional big-game hunter, organizing big-game shoots and tracking tigers for Indian princes. But soon he gave up killing wild animals for a living to turn ardently anti-killing. He has since become a fierce wildlife conservationist. Big-game hunting is one of the recurring and important themes of

Malgonkar's fiction. I asked him to describe professional hunting in the princely states.

"In India . . . Princely India, this business of shoots and arranging shoots is done on very professional lines. . . . A part of this forest was set apart, sometimes [an] entire area of the princely state is reserved only for, as far as shooting is concerned, the prince and his guests. And you wouldn't believe it that sometimes the man in charge of hunting is more important than the Prime Minister of the state. After all, he did what the ruler wanted him to in a very efficient manner. Now those particular jungles have some of the best tigers in the jungles of India. They are in very heavy forests, I know, but they are the sort of forests which are famous for tigers. You know, tigers don't live in very heavy tropical forests and these shooting boxes were built in, not only in camouflage places but even kept permanently camouflaged in the old days, and in these boxes where you could look upon them there were live buffalo baits tied up permanently for the tigers to come and kill. So if the Maharaja or the prince found a wonderful friend from America or someone like that he wanted to entertain or an official, he just took him round and looked at the tiger and said, 'Oh, this doesn't look full-grown. Shall we look at the next box?' "

In 1937 Malgonkar gave up hunting and joined Central government service as a fairly "high official." When World War II started he was "seconded" to the British Indian Army. He served for a time in the infantry, in Counter Intelligence, and in the Army's General Staff and rose to the rank of Lieutenant Colonel. He stayed on in the Army from 1942 to 1952. His *Distant Drum* (1960) deals mainly with his army experience. During these years of service in the army, Malgonkar traveled to Nepal, Indochina, Malaya, and Western Europe. He felt that army life didn't agree with him and left it in 1952 to become the representative for an American business firm in Delhi. He did not stay in business too long.

"As soon as I left the army, I was the representative for an American firm in Delhi, and they used to pay me very well; they paid me in dollars, and treated me well, too. But I found . . . that it was not a terribly satisfactory way of earning money. . . . I am not a pushing type who goes about selling things and that kind of thing, so I found things very difficult. So I gave up that job, and you know my family have been somewhat well-off by Indian standards, and they had some manganese mines which we have on our property, so I thought I could manage them. Well, to cut a long story, we then took some severe litigation with some other business people who were smarter than I was, so I took a licking and started more seriously to write."

He worked briefly on a tea plantation in the South — an experience on which he drew for his second novel, *Combat of Shadows* (1962). Malgonkar turned next to politics — his fifth career. He contested elections for the Indian parliament twice, in 1957 and 1962. He was defeated in both elections.

I asked him what his political activities were.

"Around 1956 or 1957 they started the Swantantra Party in India and I was one of the founding members of the party. Our chief was Rajaji. He is a very elderly man today, in fact, a very old man, but he was very alive and a dynamic person in those days and many of us thought that he had the right solutions to India's problems. So I and several friends joined the party and worked hard for it. But after all we don't seem to have moved with the times and we were very sadly defeated in a number of elections. I contested the first two and although the party didn't do so badly, I didn't seem to succeed and then in the last election we were wiped off the arena, almost. It is just that the people in India, by and large, don't want any rational thinking which does not offer immediate rewards, and one can't offer immediate rewards saying I'll make you rich. If the party doesn't say it, then the people don't want it."

"How would you describe your political position in American political terms?" I asked.

"In America you have just these two parties and there is so little to choose between, just the two parties. . . . There in India there is a big difference between the opinions of, for instance, the Communist Party and extreme Communist, called Communist Marxist Party, and the only way I could describe my party to you is that it is at the opposite end from the Communist Marxist Party. It would be what people here would call a Conservative . . . an Ultraconservative Party. I think that's the image the party has somehow created in America; even John Galbraith called it the John Birch Society of India."

And finally, after trying his hand at five careers, Malgonkar turned to writing as a serious career at the age of forty-six.

### III *The Art of Writing*

"Can you recall the exact moment when you decided to become a writer?" I asked.

"Well, it's a somewhat difficult question, but as I always like to answer it, the reason was mainly economic, . . . I was in the army then and I wanted to supplement my pay, which I thought it was a good thing to do by writing.

Just sit at home and write a little, and perhaps earn a little extra income and this is how it started. I was fairly old, I was about thirty-seven years old when I had my first short story published."

I asked him what really motivated him to write.

"I was paid a lot of money to write stories. I found as a military officer that I either had to give up my club and other activities or cigarettes or do something to be able to afford some luxuries. I certainly thought why not start writing to make a little extra money. So I had a friend in the All India Radio who said, 'Come on — you write a short story and we'll see if we can broadcast it over All India Radio and get you a little money.' So that became quite a regular thing afterward."

I asked him just why he wanted to write.

"It's rather like most of us stumbling into a profession in the end, you know. One doesn't consciously say at a certain age, I'm going to do this. One tries many things. Then one discovers perhaps a facility and then you go on with it, and that becomes your profession. It may have been exactly like that, it may have been a little bit of luck, if I had earned more money in business I would never have given up business, but I think it has turned out very well for me. I have landed into the profession. It's now to me a job as well as a hobby. I earn money by writing, and also it keeps me so relaxed, so occupied that I don't want to do anything at all. It's like dope, somehow, I'm in the grip of the profession now. It's rather a wonderful feeling."

Clearly an author's life has a direct bearing on what he writes. Malgonkar is among the most autobiographical of all Indian writers, hoarding, exploring, reusing, and articulating every scrap of personal experience. It is not difficult to show the intimate relationship between Malgonkar's life and writings. *Distant Drum* was about his army life; *Combat of Shadows* was about his big-game hunting. To dwell on such interconnections, however, is not to blur the distinction between the man and his works, nor to ignore the fact that a novel may contain elements which can be identified assuredly as autobiographical, but these elements may be so rearranged and transformed that they lose any specifically personal meanings to become integral with the work itself. Malgonkar draws heavily on his own experience; yet much more often than is usually allowed he transmutes this experience into enduring art.

He says:

"I feel that having started writing more or less at a very mature age, I don't have to do much research about life because I fall back on experience, you know, about army life, about shooting and hunting and the jungle life and some aspects of politics and all that which I have gone through; like our troubles with the English, for instance. I have experienced them myself so to that extent it has given me some sort of capital to draw on."

Malgonkar speaks of his *A Bend in the Ganges* as "felt experience": "Many of the situations I have described in *A Bend in the Ganges,* I have myself witnessed. And that part of Indian history I have lived through."[4]

"Is there any one character that would speak for you or would represent yourself?" I asked.

"I don't think any one character, but bits and pieces in most characters, for instance, Kiran in *Distant Drum,* Abhay in *The Princes,* Gian in *A Bend in the Ganges* and certainly not Nana, because he lived about a hundred years, or a hundred and fifty years ago."

I asked him a few somewhat inane and boring questions about the business of writing, promising not to bring up this subject again. "What are your writing habits? Do you keep a notebook? Do you always type or do you use longhand?"

"Every day at 7:30 I am at my desk bashing away at the typewriter, and that includes Sundays. I work until about 12:30 by which time I try and find excuses to leave my table, otherwise I work until I am called away to lunch, about 1:00. No, I never keep a notebook, except when I am writing about historical things. I only jot down little points, sometimes during the middle of the night, but that is to frame sentences and expressions, you know, if some way of saying something rather effectively occurs to me. I just keep a pad and scribble something on it in the middle of the night, and sometimes don't recognize what I have written in the morning. But no notes to help me with either my chapter or its characters. I always type, and then again, there is a nice story about this. When I was in the army and I started writing, naturally I had no typewriter or anything like that. I used to use my office typists; I used to pay them a little extra and work overtime. And every time I came home I had to say to my wife if we had a typewriter I could sort of bash away a story instead of doing nothing. So the next morning she went off into town and brought back a typewriter and presented it to me. I worked on that typewriter right to the time I wrote *The Princes.*"

"How many pages or words do you average — if there is any average?"

"If I want to write an article, for instance, for one of the magazines, I will do research for it early in the morning, and then start typing at about 11:00, and if I do a thousand words of rough work, I will be quite happy with it, by 1:00. Every day the same schedule, starting from about 7:30 to about 12:30. . . ."

I asked him whether he writes rapid drafts or rewrites and revises at the same time.

"It depends. For instance, in a novel like *The Princes* I wrote very rapidly and the one before that, the *Combat of Shadows* (1962), I am ashamed to say I wrote even faster. But after that, while I write just as fast, I discard just as fast, so you might say I do three or four chapters and might throw away three or four chapters. I revise and rewrite all the time, right until the draft goes to the publisher, and then I think of things to send corrections afterward."

"How many drafts do you think a particular novel may have?"

"On the average, ten. I think with *The Princes* the third one went to the publisher."

## IV  *English in India*

I asked him a few questions about English in India: "Do you feel more comfortable writing in English than in your native tongue?"

"I certainly do. Otherwise I would write in my own native tongue."

"Is that the only reason why you write in English?"

"Well, the other reason that I write in English is that I reach an audience which is more prosperous than the Indians in the Indian Republic."

"Do you always keep this abstract potential American or British reader in mind before you sit down to write?"

"Oh, very much so. Because in a book like *The Devil's Wind* if I were to write it purely for an Indian readership I wouldn't explain many things I would have to explain to an outside readership. I would take many things for granted like our religion and religious customs. And when I make references to things that have happened in history I would take them for granted. The reader knows these, being of average intelligence. But I still have to explain them to an outside audience because they still don't know much about India and it's quite natural that they shouldn't."

"Some Indian writers seem to think that when a person chooses to write in the English language he is committing some kind of self-violation. Do you feel this way?"

"Oh, certainly not. I don't think a language is any kind of a national property or anything like that — after all, the English language belongs to Australians and to the New Zealanders, too. I don't feel any sense of violation when I choose to write in English instead of in Marathi or any Indian language."

We have become aware recently that a vital international English literature has been in process of creation in Australia, New Zealand, Canada, the Philippines, Africa, the West Indies, and India. The rise of English as a literary language in these countries is the direct result of British colonization and British education. Indian contribution to this large body of literature constitutes just one band in the spectrum, or just one note in the gamut, of English literature. Malgonkar regards himself as one of the company of authors writing in English but working in traditions outside those of Britain and the United States, like Chinua Achebe, V. S. Naipaul, Patrick White, and Morley Callaghan. He believes that the astonishing capacity of the English language to express such a wide span of sensibility testifies not only to the talents of individual writers but also to the genius of the language.

I asked him if he feels that any one owns the English language.

"In fact, I don't agree with the thesis that there is any kind of ownership in the language at all. Language should be a universal thing, if anyone can master a language at all, well, good for him. Many of the German scholars, for instance, studied Sanskrit books much better than any of the Indian scholars, and they wrote grammars and various Sanskrit books more than the books that their own scholars have written. The point is that language is not national property."

He feels that we have arrived at a concept of a larger canon of English literature today. Not long ago English literature was taken to mean only the literature of the British Isles. At the turn of the century the syllabuses of English studies in our universities and colleges stretched from *Beowulf* to Virginia Woolf, never getting farther than the shores of Great Britain. Literature written in English but written outside the British Isles, even the literature of the United States, had no place in these syllabuses. No attention was paid to the emerging literatures in English of Canada, Australia, New Zealand, Philippines, West Indies, Nigeria, South Africa, and India. Now the study of English literature extends to the study of Melville, Mark Twain, Walt Whitman, and Henry James. The outstanding American writers receive critical attention. What has happened to American literature — absorption at first of a few of its major writers and then its recognition as a branch of English studies — is also happening increasingly to the literatures of other countries where English is the medium of creative expression — Canada, Australia, New Zealand, the Philippines, the West Indies, Nigeria, South Africa, and India. This process of extending and sorting out the meaning of "English literature" continues today. There is a large body of creative users of the English language outside the monolingual Empire of English, the United States and Great Britain. Indeed, scholars and critics now tend to prefer a wider term, "literature written in English," or "international English literature" as opposed to "English literature" to denote literature written both inside and outside the British Isles and the United States. Since those early constricting days, English studies have increased vastly in size and scope. "Literature written in English" may ultimately supplement or supersede the much narrower term "English literature."

I asked him if he felt he shared something in common with all English-speaking people all over the world, people living in varied cultures:

"I feel, shall we say, more akin, that I have a lot more in common with people who use the English language for writing their stuff rather than the Indians who do not use the English language. There is, as you say, the language itself, the binding factor. Apart from that I think most of English writing is done either by Americans, by Englishmen themselves, and [by] a few Indians and Australians. . . . But anything else, for instance, even in the Indian language which I can read, I find . . . [that] to follow [a] story [is] a little more troublesome, a little more difficult than to follow an English story and English thought processes."

I pressed my question. "So you do think the language itself does form a kind of commonwealth of thought and sensibility?"

"It does, indeed, yes, I was giving a talk on this subject at one of the colleges not so long ago and the point I made there was that, what's called the Indo-. Anglian writing, is an extremely special phenomenon. There is no such thing as Anglo-French literature, for instance. There is no such thing as Anglo-Korean, Anglo-Japanese, Anglo-Indonesian literature, but there is a definite area of Indo-Anglian literature and that is [that] the people who can read English or are familiar with English get a peephole into the Orient through these Indo-Anglians. Supposing you wanted to know about China. You would read a book written by the Chinese translated into English, whereas here are so many Indians writing and explaining the mysteries of the East to a Western audience, which is a peculiar phenomenon, you see, a blessing of the British Empire, almost, perhaps in disguise."

I asked him if he thought English in India was different from English in America or England.

"Let us face facts. The language we speak here is not English. At best, it is the language that was spoken by Englishmen in India twenty years ago. That was the language that we, the people of my generation, learned. Since then, English in England has gone its own way and we in India have developed our own brand of it. I am not by any means suggesting that ours is a less rich, less expressive language, only that it is not English English, just as American English or Australian English is not English English. English language is not a dead, static thing like Sanskrit or Latin, but a vigorous, living, growing thing."

Malgonkar continued:

"I'll tell you a very good story about this. I was talking to Mr. E. M. Forster at Cambridge and, just as you and I are sitting here, we were having a glass of sherry, and he said, 'Mr. Malgonkar, I want to congratulate you on the way you write English and speak it.' So I said, 'Mr. Forster, I realize, of course, that my language is twenty-five years out of date. Since you people left the country we haven't had any contact with English.' 'My dear fellow, mine is forty years out of date,' he said."

"Would you please expand on your remark about 'Indian English as a new language'?" I asked.

"As I said earlier, the language I use is very much different from American English, and English English. First, our contact with the living tongue finished about 25 years ago when the British left. Since then, in our daily conversation we speak with other Indians who don't necessarily speak the kind of English that is spoken in England. So in my novels, naturally, that difference from English English shows. But I make a very conscious effort to choose phrases and words from Indian languages which I know, if I think they are more effective than the English equivalent that I know. I feel that the experiment sometimes works. Sometimes it doesn't."

In an interview with Dr. M. Fisher Malgonkar said:

"There are fourteen different kinds of Indian English, whereas you have just one kind of American English or Australian English. But in India, there are many different languages, and they all impose their own speech rhythms, their own phrases, onto English. The English that is spoken, shall we say, in the Punjab is not necessarily understood by the English-speaking people in the South, in Kerala, for instance."[5]

"Are there some Indianisms perhaps like Americanisms?" I asked.

"I will tell you this, there is a Marathi phrase that has application like 'a washed grain of rice.' I thought it was a good expression and I put it [in, ]you know, to show how clean it was. Originally, I used to be a little scared about putting Indianisms into my novels, because I knew that they were intended mainly for Americans and Englishmen, but in my latest book, I have deliberately used many Indianisms, taking my cue from people like Kipling for instance; you may know that his dialogue is full of Indianisms, so I said, why shouldn't I introduce my Indianisms?"

"In other words, when you write, you don't consciously attempt to imitate British English or American English but you try to use English as you know it?" I asked.

"And as effectively as I can write it. But mind you, that has to bear with my own limitations of the language. I cannot write English as perhaps E. M. Forster writes it, for instance. They write it beautifully. I haven't got the facility nor the command of so many words. That's why, to get over my limitations, perhaps I try to bring in Marathi words and phrases."

Malgonkar does not think there is any future for Indian writing in English. He says:

"I don't think it's got any future at all. . . . There isn't much English being taught these days. The sort of English we do write now-a-days is not going to be written even ten years from now, the sort of English that you people in England and America will understand."[6]

## V  *Influences on Malgonkar*

I ask him if any English and American writers had any influence on his writings.

"I don't think there was any one novelist, but I have always acknowledged a debt to the American novelist John P. Marquand, who I thought wrote from my sort of background and about my sort of people. I made a very deep study of his novels and of his craft. He has a great deal of polish, which I don't find in much American writing, and if anyone has influenced my style, it has been him."

"What specific aspects of his work did appeal to you most?"

"He wrote as a learned man about other learned men. He wrote about a social class which was not just an ordinary class; he wrote about the highly educated, well-to-do Americans doing the sort of job that well-to-do Americans do. Then he wrote about the army which again is a background very familiar to me. And he wrote about very civilized people doing very civilized things. Which is what I feel I do well. Since then, I have started writing a lot about violence and somewhat uncivilized things, too. But in the craft of telling the story, he has influenced me a lot."

He went on to develop his ideas:

"John P. Marquand had a great influence on me because I liked his literary style, his thought processes. I could identify completely with the way his heart was, with the little failures, with the little vanities and everything. That's the only novelist, American novelist, I read more deeply, and I can sort of quote passages from him in everything he has written, either short stories or long novels. There are others I have read merely as entertainment and the people I have liked apart from the very big names like Hemingway, Faulkner, and others. I like Truman Capote. I used to like Robert Ruark and Steinbeck, certainly one of my greatest favorites. He is a wonderful craftsman and you know that's the sort of thing I have to depend on, craftsmanship in telling a story because whatever we say, the language is not ours and our limitations come to the fore. It's been grafted on us and we have adopted it. I have to depend entirely on my skill to push forward the plot, on my craftsmanship as a novelist; I think and I appreciate when I see it in someone else, like in E. M. Forster or Steinbeck."

Malgonkar discusses in detail the literary influences that shaped him in his article in *The Times Literary Supplement.* He pored over Dickens, Bennett, H. G. Wells, G. K. Chesterton, and Shaw, but they remained "outsiders."

For they wrote mainly about England and on English way of life, unfamiliar subjects to those of us who knew England only through officials of the Empire and planters and soldiers and the box wallahs. . . . And so gradually, the writers who became front rank favorites were those who mainly wrote about things which were recognizable at first hand.

And that brought on the full spate of writers who wrote about the East and particularly about India, from Meadows Taylor to Maud Diver. Kipling . . . side by side with Somerset Maugham, Joseph Conrad, E. M. Forster. . . . The only tangible influence I am aware of is that these authors have helped me to formulate my own idea of what constitutes a good novel. The one factor that I find common in all these writers to whom I happen to be specially attached is that they are excellent story-tellers. Their novels are well constructed, all dramatic, and they are not afraid of incident; above all, they entertain. . . . I do strive deliberately and hard, to tell a story well; and I revel in incident, in improbabilities, in unexpected twists. . . .[7]

Malgonkar admires greatly Kipling and E. M. Forster.

"To my mind no one has transformed the full, stinging flavour of the Indian peasant's language into English as Kipling has, and no other author has shown such a deep (almost embarrassingly deep) understanding of the character of the educated Indian as E. M. Forster has.[8]

I asked him to comment on E. M. Forster's *A Passage to India* (1924).

"It is a work of great art, and I always treat it from many different points of view. Its theme is that of friendship between the white man and the dark man and he establishes, in fact, he says it again and again, long before the word become fashionable, that unless there is affection there cannot be friendship. He says, in so many words, that understanding is not enough, good government is not enough, you want affection. And that was a requirement which is quite impossible under those conditions. The British didn't understand us, we didn't understand them, the conditions were absolutely foreign, absolutely hostile to any understanding. Then again, there is another point that he does establish, this point is, in the words of his characters, 'so long as you are ruling us, we shall never be friends.' And that has been told in such a wonderful manner by a writer who did not spend much more than eleven months in India in his two trips. His understanding of India and Indian characters is almost embarrassingly true. When he says so and so said such and such a thing and analyzes and leaves open the mental processes it somehow brings on a feeling of quite acute shame and embarrassment in someone like myself to say, 'How can this man look deep into our minds and consciences, like that?' And thirdly, I like his very subtle humor. I admire him very greatly."

"Do you admire any other English writer who deals with India?" I asked.

"I admire Paul Scott. . . . He knows one particular aspect of India very well. And that was the India during the war. And he knows one side of it very well which was the side that was seen by the Indian army, or the British army in those days. He was a member of the British army, and to that extent he has got it more correctly, more truly, more honestly than many Englishmen or foreigners have got. He just by coincidence stayed with me two months ago and I saw him again in London about two weeks ago."

## VI  *Of Other Indian Writers in English*

We turned to Indian novelists in English. "Do you read Indian novelists in English? Is there anyone who is your favorite?" I asked.

"I don't go out of my way to read them. If it comes my way, I certainly read them, I don't reject them. But there are so few of them, it's very difficult to find the time to read a novel because it is written by an Indian. I think I know all of them. I know R. K. Narayan, I know K. Singh, I have met Desani, I know his work. But there is K. Singh who I like as a person, and he's a great friend of mine. Well, I am afraid I have no favorites among them. I think the most prolific among them is Narayan. He is a very good writer and writes very sincerely about his part of the world, without, to my mind, introducing artificial values, as most of us do, and he had a very good following in this country. He is a good novelist and a good storyteller, to my mind. He is a good craftsman. He tells the story and he creates good characters and he doesn't dabble too much in the plotless kind of novel."

I mentioned Nirad C. Chaudhury's *The Autobiography of an Unknown Indian*. Malgonkar's answer showed a hint of feeling against Nirad Chaudhury.

"Chaudhury is an oddball, you know. He is an Anglophile to the nth degree as you might see from the dedication of his book *Autobiography of an Unknown Indian*. Just see his dedication. He feels that the Englishmen are gods, and because he knows their language well enough and knows something of their history, he is only a demigod and of all other Indians, only those who were made by the English, given life and created by the English, are the best Indians."

The following is the epigraph that Malgonkar dislikes very much even though his own *Distant Drum* is not completely free from Anglophilia.

To the memory of the British Empire in India which conferred subjecthood on us but withheld citizenship; to which yet everyone of us threw out the challenge: "Civis Britannicus Sum" because all that was good and living within us was made, shaped, and quickened by the same British rule.[9]

He admires Raja Rao, another Indian writer of repute:

"He's a very good writer. He can use English perhaps better than most other Indian writers. He uses the language very well, and he mixes up his Indian linguistic patterns and the English language — and I think he has a good knowledge of the French language too. He synthesizes all these in a very good medium.[10]

Malgonkar does not regard Kamala Markandaya and Prawer Jhabvala as Indian writers:

"I don't think [they[ . . . qualify to be Indian writers at all. Mrs. Jhabvala is not Indian, and Kamala Markandaya left India about, what, twenty-five years ago. So to that extent, one was born Indian and therefore should be called Indian; one has adopted India as her country and therefore should be called Indian. I think they're not very genuinely Indian writers at all."[11]

## VII   *Screenplays and Books in Progress*

Our conversation turned to the present and future. "What sort of work are you engaged in now?" I asked.

"I do all kinds of work, because being a professional writer, I can't pick and choose too much. I do a certain amount of ghostwriting, I write for the Indian movies, scripts and stories, I write articles for weekly or monthly magazines, particularly a rather prestigious current magazine called *Orientations,* which is published in Hong Kong. Then I write for one or two of the Indian magazines, and I am always, naturally enough, being a novelist, thinking of my next novel."

Malgonkar has written several screenplays for Indian movies. One of them, *Spy in Amber,* was published in India (Orient Paperbacks) as a novel. The work of transcription was mainly done by Sunita Malgonkar, his daughter.

I asked him to describe his work for the movies.

"Our entertainment is so restricted — only to the films, and the population as you know, is enormous. So those who produce films in India are really like kings, like what Hollywood moguls were before the Second World War. So it's a very thriving industry. . . . The long and short of it is that the movie industry is not only alive but it's filled with money. . . . I know a screenplay's not like a novel — a film story you finish in two to three months and it pays about three or four times as much as a novel does. . . . My work is very much easier there because I just do it in English, and they have got their own people to translate these things and put the dialogue into Hindi. But actually I'm engaged in one now and I'm going back to London just for that — this gentleman who is a friend of mine asked me to write a movie story based on the Indians in England. You know there are all sorts of difficulties and troubles and tensions and that kind of thing. So I'm going to spend two to three weeks in London getting material for it and then I'll go back to India and work on the story, and I hope he'll make a movie of it. But this he intends to make in English as well as Hindi.

The novel itself is a form which I feel is not very rewarding in terms of monetary returns, so to keep going, most writers have to have something else out there — some teach in colleges, some, perhaps, work on television networks or that kind of thing. My own thing is that I write books of history now and then, commissioned books, and also I do screenplays. So I am now doing one based on the life of Indians living in England."

"What are you planning for the future?" I asked.

"I have got a novel three-fourths formed, or perhaps even nine-tenths formed. It's a novel which I think says everything that I want said. Whether the publishers think that everything has been said in it which an author should say, I don't know because these things are a matter of dialogue between the publishers, editor, and the author. Whatever form it is in, it is at the moment with both my publishers in London and New York. Correct form would be to say it is with my agent, and I do feel that during the next year or so I will arrive at a form of a novel which will be mutually acceptable both to the publisher and myself. It might be published sometime in 1973 or 1974. The new novel will be all about the takeover of Goa by India told from the point of the Goanese."

I asked him whether he looked forward to writing more books.

"Not a lot. Certainly three or four more novels, and perhaps three or four other works, one or two books of history."

I asked him if he thought of dealing with the India-China War in a novel.

"Yes, I am very glad you asked that. I started a novel on the Chinese invasion very soon after the Chinese invasion occurred. And I wrote the full novel, but I am not very happy with it. I'll tell you why I was not very happy with it. Because I had to write it very tongue-in-cheek. Because Nehru was still alive, the advisers who had led him into this tremendous bungle against the Chinese suffered a very humiliating defeat from a force which we then at least did not consider to be equal to that of the Indian army. I was going to bring out all the dirt, and I couldn't; I would have had to write it tongue-in-cheek. Now I don't know if the time for it is still there. Many facts which could not have been revealed then can be revealed now. For instance, the military defeat. Menon, our defense minister, and Nehru . . . and his advisers were almost directly responsible for, were almost criminally responsible for, the humiliations we suffered and the defeat at the Chinese hands. This could be set down very nicely in a novel, and I had attempted it and the story is nearly complete; now perhaps one of these days I'll polish it. All the things that have happened in my life I have written about, not things read from books."

Malgonkar's publishers have another of his novels which is a character study of a landowning politician in a country district.

Malgonkar has visited the United States four times, in 1963, 1964, 1970, and 1972. During these visits he lectured at many colleges and universities. During the fall semester of 1972 he spent three days at Lock Haven State College, lecturing on English in India and on his novels. The following are the titles of some of his lectures on the campuses in the United States: "E. M. Forster's India"; "The Last days of the Maharajas"; "Indian English, a New Language"; "Indo-American Relations Today"; "Communism in India"; "The Rise of Violence in India and The Vanishing Jungle." The list testifies to his wide range of interests. He is not an ivory-tower novelist, but one who continues to participate in the political and social life of India. As a public speaker and conversationalist what is most striking about Malgonkar's conversation is his command of the English language: his spoken sentences are as precise and rounded as his written sentences. He never gives the impression of searching for a word. He talks quickly, confidently, eagerly yet unaffectedly — obviously enjoying it. His voice and manner are warm and gentle. No transcript taken from the tape could catch the subtleties of voice which give life and point to many of his remarks. Nor could a printed page convey his clipped British accents.

Malgonkar is his own critic and a sound one at that. I asked him whether he thought highly of all his works.

"The way to describe it is like this, that all my work is the best that I can do. I know that it has to be uneven, but I put my best into everything that I produce, even if you want an article, or you want a paid thing, a commissioned thing that you want me to do, a ghostwriting, I will work at it just as hard as if it were my own work."

"When you look back, do you think your first book is not as good as your latest book?" I asked.

"It always happens, indeed, because any rewriting, to my mind, always improves things. If you have the time, like some authors or most authors seem to have, one should never publish a novel, but go on working on them forever and forever until they are published after your death. I find that a book like *A Bend in the Ganges,* I could have, to great advantage, cut down about 30,-000 words from it and made perhaps a better book of it. Now I think so."

Malgonkar continues to begin work every day at 7:30 A.M. He lives with his wife, daughter, and his dog Busty in Jagalbet and grows coconuts, oranges, and mangoes.

## CHAPTER 2

# The Growth of a Novelist:
# Distant Drum *and*
# Combat of Shadows

MALGONKAR'S literary career began in 1960 when he published his first novel, *Distant Drum* (1960), in Bombay. He had come out of the army after having risen to the rank of Lieutenant Colonel. His second novel, *Combat of Shadows* (1962), was published in London in 1962 when he was forty-nine years old. He had by then given up another career as a professional big-game hunter. It is interesting to note these facts because these novels, like his later novels, have a great deal to say about life in the army and about hunting. What is most striking about these early novels is not the quality of his writing — they are not his best novels though there are some fine passages in them — but the great value they have of introducing the major and minor themes of all his novels. He has written five novels including the two mentioned above. The other three are *The Princes* (1963), *A Bend in the Ganges* (1964), and *The Devil's Wind* (1972).

It is difficult to deny that the five works, taken as a whole, constitute a consistent and thoughtful statement about life; they present a particular "vision of life" — always the mark of a fine artist.

What do these novels have in common and what can they tell us about Malgonkar's vision of life?

The works of novelists often have a unity that tempts the critic to look for a central theme, even a controlling concept or symbol, that focuses their vision of life. I find all the novels of Malgonkar, taken together, to be concerned with a number of themes, somewhat generally stated in the early novels, but developed at length in the later ones. Some themes are somewhat sketchily developed in *Distant Drum* and *Combat of Shadows,* though the recurrent themes of his fiction are all there. The early novels should be read closely not so much for their accomplishment as for their promise; they tell something about the general progress and development of his art. We see in them a novelist feeling his way, exploring his materials, to reach a level of mastery which he achieves only in his later works.

To consider his novels chronologically and to look at their themes briefly would be to see his literary art in progress. The Table on the next page will make the pattern clear. All his novels, which are in a sense closely interconnected, are concerned with five themes; it is as if each book was a chord or segment of a total situation always existing in his mind. To put it another way, all the separate works are like blocks of marble from the same quarry; they share the veins and faults of the mother rock. Malgonkar seems to be telling the same story but with new details and variations. A major-theme - minor-theme index may be developed on a numerical scale from 1 (major theme) to 5 (minor theme).

The figures of this table can be used only as a rough indicator of the themes. However useful such figures may be they are mostly just isolated facts of limited value in critical analysis. They tell little about how successful the novelist has been in handling these themes. Nevertheless, we can see that Malgonkar's major theme in the early novels — *Distant Drum* and *Combat of Shadows* — is "Indo-British relationships at the personal level" but in his later novels this very theme becomes a minor one — *The Princes* (5), *A Bend in the Ganges* (4), and *The Devil's Wind* (4).

On the other hand "History of India" is a relatively minor theme in the early novels — *Distant Drum* (3) and *Combat of Shadows* (5) — but it becomes a major theme in the later novels — *The Princes* (1), *A Bend in the Ganges* (1), and *The Devil's Wind* (1). The periods of history presented are indicated in parentheses.

Similarly, early novels anticipate the theme of "initiation" which is developed at length in the later novels. Another interesting point is that the theme of "hunting" drops out of later novels.

As one novel leads into another other similarities become apparent: all the protagonists are young men; all the novels are set in particular parts of India, generally northern India; and all the novels deal with periods of Indian history concerned with India's struggle for independence. The young men go through more or less the same period in all novels (except *The Devil's Wind*) in more or less the same geographical area in India. What goes on in one novel, when and where it goes on, is repeated, developed, and underscored in another novel.

When we examine the novels to try to get at the "figure in the carpet," then, the two early novels can be seen to present the germ of

## TABLE OF THEMES

| Themes | Distant Drum (1960) | Combat of Shadows (1962) | The Princes (1963) | A Bend in The Ganges (1964) | The Devil's Wind (1972) |
|---|---|---|---|---|---|
| Indo-British Relationships at the Personal Level | 1 | 1 | 5 | 4 | 4 |
| Initiation | 2 | 4 | 2 | 2 | 2 |
| History of India | 3 (1938-50) | 5 (1938-40) | 1 (1938-48) | 1 (1938-47) | 1 (1857-58) |
| Relationships between Men and Women | 4 | 3 | 3 | 3 | 3 |
| Hunting | 5 | 2 | 4 | | |

Malgonkar's fictional program. Colonel Kiran Garud of *Distant Drum* points forward all the way to Captain Abhayraj of *The Princes*. The same historical period is recreated in *Distant Drum* and in *The Princes*. In the early novels Malgonkar is groping and developing as an artist toward his forte which he discovers only in his later novels. He is at his best in his later novels when he deals with recent Indian history and initiation themes. The other three themes he either drops or deals with only sketchily in his later novels, as we will see.

## I   Distant Drum (1960)

The action of Malgonkar's first novel is relatively simple. The story is divided into three parts: "The Regiment," "The Staff," and "Active Service." Lieutenant Colonel Kiran Garud, the protagonist, is an officer of the 4th Satpuras of the Indian army, otherwise known as the Fighting Fourth or Fighting Tigers. The focus is on his experiences in Raniwada as the Commanding Officer of the Regiment, in New Delhi as a member of the staff of the Directorate of War Plans, and on the Kashmir front as a Commanding Officer of the 2nd Satpuras. The action covers not only the period from August, 1949, to March, 1950, but also, on a deeper level, an earlier period from

1938 to 1949 when Kiran rose from the rank of Second Lieutenant to that of Lieutenant Colonel after going through the Burma War in 1942 and winning a Military Cross for "exemplary devotion to duty in the field of battle."

"The Regiment" begins with Kiran's visit to Shingargaon in August, 1949, for the Infantry Commanders Conference. When he goes to meet his friend Arun Sanwal he is introduced to Miss Bina Sonal. He finds her very attractive and likes her grace, poise, perfume, and the way she laughed. She tells him that she had seen him in Raniwada almost every day on the tennis courts with Mrs. Margot Medley. On his way back to Raniwada after the conference he keeps thinking of both Bina and Margot Medley, wife of Major Robert Medley, with whom he had had an affair during the war.

Kiran's memories about Margot take him back to the tennis games in Raniwada before the war and to a happy night he had spent with her in her flat in Calcutta in 1944 when her husband was away. She was good-looking, with even features, a trim, leggy, well-preserved figure, and a wonderfully glowing skin. Bob Medley who discovered them together next morning had gone away in a daze and shot himself to death. Kiran thinks that he was responsible for Bob Medley's suicide though Margot took it coolly.

At Shingargaon Kiran's friends had reminded him of another episode in which he had "ticked off" Colonel Manners. All the Indian officers had admired him for his courage. Lieutenant Colonel Manners commanded the 4th Satpuras for a brief period in 1938. Kiran at that time was only a Second Lieutenant. The incident had taken place in the Mess. Colonel Manners who never liked India or Indians said, after having had a lot to drink; " 'If it came to that, I am not at all sure that the men of this bloody regiment would stand the test of loyalty.' " (17). Completely upset by this remark, Kiran addressed his commanding officer from the other side of the room; " 'Will you permit me to leave The Mess, Sir, since you appear to doubt the loyalty of my regiment' " (18).

In Raniwada as Commanding Officer Kiran clashes with a local political boss, Lala Vishnu Saran Dev, Chairman of the District Congress Committee, who belligerently demands the regiment's Shamiana for a reception planned for a minister. Kiran tells him plainly that it cannot be used for a political show. At the end of "The Regiment" Kiran is assigned to the Directorate of War Plans in New Delhi.

"The Staff" begins with Kiran's arrival in New Delhi. He gets in touch with Bina Sonal, who works for the All India Radio Station, and takes her to a dance at a club. They meet often and their relationship deepens and develops while her father, Gobind Ram Sonal, an influential secretary in the government, is making plans for her marriage to a rich young man, Arvind Mathur. When Mr. Sonal tells his daughter of his plans she tells him flatly that she is not going to marry Arvind. He does his best to reason with her but Bina continues to raise objections. She is in love with Kiran and does not want to marry anyone else. Mr. Sonal, however, does not think well of people in the army because they are badly paid and are shunted all over the country to places where they can't take their families.

Mr. Sonal, then, sure of Bina's interest in Kiran, proceeds to get him transferred from New Delhi to the operational area of Kashmir. On the day Kiran receives the transfer orders Mr. Sonal visits him in the mess lounge and explains why he thought it would be expedient to have him transferred.

"Well, my daughter's marriage is more or less settled, with someone whom I consider entirely suitable. And I don't want anything to upset my plans. . . . I feel terribly guilty about it. And I can assure you that as soon as things get straightened out, within two or three months say, I can arrange to have you brought back to Delhi." (193)

Besides the developing love story of Kiran and Bina, "The Staff" includes some flashbacks in which Kiran remembers British officers he admires most — "Bull" Hampton, Ropey Booker, and Bertie Howard. Bull Hampton, a short, thickset man, had gone into Burma with the Satpuras. When the 4th reached the Twin-Pagoda Hill, Bull led his company in an attack, shouting the famous words: "Come on Jawans; Tigers don't live forever."

Although the attack was a stupid blunder, the spirit in which Bull launched the attack mattered most to the Satpuras.

Bull had succeeded in smashing through an attitude of mind which the Satpuras and indeed most of the troops then in Burma were beginning to develop: an attitude of "sit and wait and let the enemy take the initiative." Bull had chosen to take the offensive; that was all that mattered. This attack,

game leg and all, had all the romance of an old-fashioned Cavalry Charge.
(129)

Ropey Booker, the commanding officer, lean and handsome, loved
and revered by most of the men, was regarded as the one man above
all men who most nearly lived up to the code of the Satpuras. He was
Kiran's hero: "Whenever Kiran was confronted with a tricky situation, he always tried to think out what a British CO would have done
in his place." (52). Ropey, Kiran remembers, loved his Jawans; he
played hockey with them, and he even spent a few days of leave every
year in the village home of a retired Subedar Major of the 4th, living
with the family the life of an Indian Villager.

Bertie Howard and Kiran were close friends during the Burma
Campaigns. In 1938 when Kiran joined the 4th Satpuras, Lieutenant
Hubert Howard was Senior Subaltern of the battalion. As Senior
Subaltern Bertie had often taken Kiran in hand, taught him the
regimental customs and mess etiquette. Kiran admires his ability to
"dish it out." Bertie also brought memories of their experiences during the battle of the Sittang Bridge in 1941. The Japanese had con-
verged in a westerly pincer movement on the Sittang Bridge. The
bridge, the only one of its kind, spanned the wide and treacherous
Sittang river. In the battle that took place for the bridge, both Captain Kiran and Colonel Howard had performed many individual
deeds of valor and sacrifice. Though the Satpuras suffered a crushing
defeat, the battle still remains the highest point of their active service.

"Active Service" begins with Kiran commanding a battalion in action on the Kashmir front in December, 1949. It is with an eager
spirit, the spirit of a soldier setting out on active service, that he
reports to the Headquarters of the 395th Brigade of which his new
battalion, the 2nd Satpuras formed a part. The enemy battalion facing him, the 37th Baluch, is commanded by his friend, Abdul Jamal,
now an officer in the Pakistan army. Abdul, he remembers, was one
of the 4th Satpuras with him in Burma and had even saved his life in
September, 1947, at the time of the Delhi riots. They were close
friends; Kiran used to spend a part of his annual leave with Abdul.
Kiran expects to defend his position in Kashmir, to lead his men into
an attack without any other thought in mind except that of winning.
Unfortunately, however, a ceasefire is declared. The Brigade Commander announces: " 'With effect from the midnight of December
31st all fighting, all along the line, is to stop. A ceasefire line has been
agreed upon' " (221).

Kiran, at this point, on the last day of 1949, is surprised to receive a telegram from Abdul Jamal, which reads:

From Abdul
To Jacko
Happy New Year.

Kiran sends a suitable reply after much hesitation.

From Jacko
To Abdul
Same to you stop what about a celebration stop if you agree RV Bushy Top Tree Map Ref 435684 Repeat 435684 At 1700 hrs this day. (225)

A reply comes back within half an hour — Abdul agrees to meet and celebrate the New Year. Kiran takes a bottle of champagne and meets Abdul under the Bushy Top Tree. They empty glasses rather hurriedly shouting "Come on Jawans; Tigers don't live forever!" After a few minutes of nervous conversation they smash glasses, laugh awkwardly, and walk back to their respective camps without a single backward glance.

This meeting with Abdul Jamal gets Kiran into trouble with his Superior officers. The Division Commander feels that Kiran should not remain in command. Kiran applies for leave and goes to Delhi for the Satpura Reunion for which Ropey Booker had come from England. He tells General Torgal that he was prepared to face a trial by a Court Martial. The General, however, only warns him not to let this happen again.

In March General Ballur asks Kiran to take over the 4th Satpuras again and make them a Brigade of Guards. Kiran is happy to go back to Raniwada. On his way to Raniwada he stops in Delhi to meet Bina. He meets her and proposes marriage.

"You know, Raniwada has a vast house for the CO . . ."
"Is that where you are going?"
"Yes, Raniwada, on a special posting. And the house is called The Flag Staff House [and] has . . . eight bedrooms and a bandstand in the garden. . . ." (257)

The novel begins in Raniwada, moves to New Delhi, Burma, and Kashmir, and returns to Raniwada.

It is clear, from the bare outline given above, that of the five recurring themes, the two major themes of *Distant Drum,* though not dealt with at great length, are "the Indo-British relationships at a personal level" and "the education or initiation of Kiran Garud." The British Indian Army was a club in which the Britishers and Indians got along splendidly. Indian officers, in Malcolm Muggeridge's words, are the last true Englishmen; they were at times more English than the English themselves. Kiran Garud's greatest ambition was to become very much like Ropey Booker; he always strives to live up to the code that the British had introduced. Kiran even turns down a lucrative job Ropey Booker offers in business for the sake of the principles of the Satpuras. "My word! Playing the Pukka Sahib with Ropey!" (252) was General Ballur's comment on this.

Malgonkar's treatment of the personal relationships between the British and Indian officers is one of the most interesting aspects of the book. He shows nothing of the skepticism that E. M. Forster had presented in his *A Passage to India* (1924) about the possibility of genuine friendship between Britishers and Indians. E. M. Forster's concluding comment in his novel was: "No, not yet," and the Sky said, "No, not there." Rudeness, wickedness, arrogance, insensitivity of the kind shown by Mrs. Turton or by Ronny Heaslop are not seen in Malgonkar's British officers. Almost all of them — Ropey Booker, Bull Hampton, Girgut Jones, Bertie Howard, Robert Medley, and others — show friendliness, courtesy, and respect for their Indian colleagues. All except Colonel Manners who

"did not like India or Indians, and he made no secret of it. . . . if he said that the Indians were thoroughly uncivilized, that they wouldn't be able to rule themselves in a thousand years, that their religion, their art, their music, were barbaric, the CO was merely expressing an opinion . . . and when he said things like 'Gandhi is a quack and Nehru an utter charlatan, and the only thing to do with all sedition-mongers is to put them against a wall. . . .' " (16)

Indians, too, show friendliness, courtesy, and respect for their British colleagues; they hold them in high esteem. All except Kamala Kant are anglophiles.

"To me, no Britisher is all right; they are all bastards," he said. "You remember how in the old days we used to say that there were only two kinds of Englishmen: swines and bloody swines." (243)

Despite Col. Manners and Col. Kamala Kant, anti-British feeling and anti-Indian feeling at a time when Indians were struggling to wrest freedom from their British rulers were kept at the minimum. Malgonkar's main purpose was to celebrate Indian "army life," a life without animosity and bitterness between the rulers and the ruled. Indians and Britishers emerge from Malgonkar's novel as genuine friends, friends capable of sacrifice and love for one another. As the CO said, " 'In this Regiment, we are, first and foremost, gentlemen. No Satpura officer ever consciously does anything that would hurt the Regiment's *izzat* ["honor"]' "

Another important and continuous theme of *Distant Drum* is the initiation of Kiran Garud, his movement from "Bum Wart" to CO of the 4th Satpuras in the British Indian Army. The novel records his growing up. We follow the hero through his experiences, his attempts to prove himself. This notion of maturing growth that can only occur through encounter with experience is one of Malgonkar's primary themes; it is treated in all his novels. The drawing of Kiran is very sketchy as yet, compared with later portraits of Abhay in *The Princes* (1963) or of Gian in *A Bend in the Ganges* (1964). And the experiences of young manhood which shape Kiran shape Abhay and Gian as well even though in *Distant Drum* we are only given simple surfaces, not profound depths of character. Kiran's growth between 1938, when he joins the 4th Satpuras as a Second Lieutenant, and 1950, when he returns from the Kashmir front to Raniwada as CO with his bride Bina Sonal, consists of six stages. I will deal with them briefly one by one.

First, Kiran as Second Lieutenant in the regiment. He begins as a "Bum Wart" in 1938. The "Bum Warts" were Second Lieutenants who had to put in eighteen months of grueling training before they could qualify "for being promoted to 'Warts.' " The "Bum Warts" were often treated as dirt and less than dirt by their superior officers. A Senior Subaltern was supposed to "take in hand" the Second Lieutenants, teach them the regiment's customs and mess etiquette. Sometimes Bertie Howard would take Kiran in hand. Once Bertie took Kiran to task for not playing "Freda," a game played at the billiard table, with zest. He says:

". . . What do you think this is? A bloody funeral? . . . Then why the blazes don't you show that you are enjoying it? Don't you realize that there are outsiders present? Guests of the mess. You are a host. Bloody fine host you make! For God's sake learn to act as if you are enjoying it. (124)

Kiran realizes that it was his business to sparkle at guest nights whether he liked it or not. Higher officers often insulted and made the "Bum Warts" angry. Bull Hampton, for instance, once did not allow Kiran to sit down and drink a lemon squash even though Kiran was thoroughly exhausted after marching miles for exercise. Kiran was asked to return to the men who had marched with him and inspect their feet. When Kiran returns after foot-inspection he is asked to go and water the mules. "Watering mules is a hellish business and it took Kiran a full hour before they were finished. 'I hope the swine doesn't find something else for me to do now,' he said to himself, as he walked into the ante-room for the third time that afternoon" (133).

In the beginning Kiran, too, went about feeling angry and bitter like all "Bum Warts." It was only later that he began to realize that all this was part of the process of putting him through the paces, "a process of hardening you up, of increasing your resistance to stress; it was all an essential part of your grounding as an officer and a gentleman, fit to command the King's men. . . . It was not merely a matter of hard training. . . . It was even more, a process of cutting you down to size, as they put it, of making you learn how 'to take it' . . . " (71). Kiran learned not only "to take it" in the right spirit but also to "dish it out."

Learning that part took a hell of a long time, though, because it was one of the most difficult things in life to blow up someone and still leave him with the impression that there was nothing personal in it. But after you had mastered that, you were fit for any command.

Kiran, then, trained earlier at the Military Academy in Dehra-Dun, receives further education at the regiment from the British officers. They turn him into almost another British officer. His total devotion to the British Indian Army Code leads him even to "tick off" Col. Manners when the regiment's loyalty was questioned, as we have seen. Later, as CO, Kiran turns down a lucrative job in business offered by Ropey Booker, his British hero. Ropey "in his mind had always represented his ideal of a military commander" (237).

Second, Kiran does active service in Burma and Kashmir battlefields. Kiran goes through two campaigns, wins a Military Cross for "exemplary devotion to duty in the field of battle," and is posted as CO of a battalion in action on the Kashmir front, although he does not get a chance to fight the enemy in Kashmir. He displays his courage and leadership at these places. Kiran's first attack against a Japanese position in a Burma jungle was a success; he had even killed a man in hand-to-hand fighting. Here in Burma he participates in the fighting for the Sittang Bridge, sees Ropey Booker in action, admires and learns his cold professional manner under extreme stress. In Kashmir he was responsible for a front of nearly a thousand yards but all fighting had to stop when a ceasefire was declared. It was then that he decides to meet Abdul Jamal obeying a higher order of friendship and loyalty.

Third, Kiran is initiated into sexual knowledge by Margot Medley. When Margot finds Kiran diffident and awkward she tells him flatly, " 'Don't ever tell a woman you are sorry you kissed her. . . . Now you just go up and bring out your toothbrush and pyjamas. . . ' " (26). This is how they spend a night together in Calcutta during the war. He is no longer the same after that night.

Fourth, Kiran discovers the value of friendship and loyalty with Abdul Jamal during the Hindu-Moslem riots in New Delhi in 1947. Nearly thirty thousand Moslem refugees had taken shelter in a mosque. Hindus and Moslems were massacring one another in madness outside the mosque. Kiran and Abdul go into the mosque. The mob roars "kill him," for Kiran is a Hindu. Abdul intervenes effectively and saves Kiran's life. For some days the two work together, helping the wounded and maintaining the curfew. "What stood out magnificently secure in that holocaust was the fact that although they belonged to two opposing communities crazed with vengeance and thirsting for blood, he and Abdul had been able to work together in the closest accord, their loyalties to each other absolutely unruptured by that incessant strain" (218). Kiran never forgets the incident in the mosque.

Fifth, Kiran as CO in Raniwada refuses to yield to political pressure. As we have seen, Kiran flatly tells Saran Dev that the Shamiana is not meant for political show. He is firm, precise, and confident as CO; he has learned to "dish it out." He takes his professional responsibilities seriously and regards himself as privileged to be an officer of the army with an extra responsibility of building up the coming generation of officers. It was in this spirit that he does not accept Ropey Booker's offer. He tells Ropey:

"We are the privileged ones, those who have been taught by people like you, and who have gone through a war. . . Now the new, post-war officers are beginning to finish their training and are coming into the army. . . . I feel it is up to us, the old guard, to mold them — just as you and your contemporaries molded us. . . . It is a sort of debt we have towards those who are now coming. . . . (239)

And finally, Kiran makes the commitment of love and offers to marry Bina. He is no longer frightened of marital responsibility. He had never paid attention to her in Raniwada tennis courts when he was playing with Margot. When introduced to her at Shingargaon he was attracted to her by her poise. He felt "it would be fun playing tennis with her; much more fun kissing her" (11). But when he was posted to Delhi he almost forgot her. He sees her at Mansingh's party unexpectedly and renews his relationship. When he meets her or takes her to parties he gives the impression of being an uncertain and unsure person. It is always the regiment that is above everything else in his life — even Bina Sonal cannot distract him from his devotion to the life of the army. He shows his readiness to pack up and go to the Kashmir front when Bina's father gets him transferred to Kashmir. Bina herself tells him of her lack of interest in the young man her father had chosen for her. Kiran draws her close to him, kisses her, and says that he is terribly in love with her. That's all. But later when her father explains the transfer he tells him, " 'We always finish off our own tigers . . . I am prepared to go along with you. . . . My career to me is more important than anything else — more important than your daughter' " (193 - 96).

Kiran then leaves for the Kashmir front without a word to Bina. Weeks later when in New Delhi for the Satpura Reunion he calls Bina on a sudden impulse and meets her. He still talks of his having commanded an active battalion and of Bina's approaching wedding. Bina once again takes the initiative and helps him to think through his priorities:

"Jacko, do you still love me?" . . .
"I have already broken my word to your father," he said. "It was all a mistake, my asking you to see me. Let's go back."
    "I asked you a question," she said, still looking hard at him. . . .
    "I know you did. The answer is, I do. But I don't see the point of going into all this now. It can only make things worse."
    "Then I am not going to marry Arvind Mathur. . . . It is so simple, really . . . . I have never stopped loving you; only I doubted whether a man like you was capable of falling in love; I mean really and completely in love. I have often wondered if you were not deliberately preventing yourself from . . . liking anyone." . . . (248)

This straight talk was the turning point in his growth. Next time he is in New Delhi, on his way to Raniwada, he rings up Bina, invites her for a drive, tells her of his new job at Raniwada, and asks her to marry him. " 'I can never tell you how much I love you. How much I have missed you . . . these last three months have been torture' " (257).

Besides personal relationships between the British and Indian officers of the Indian Army and Kiran's initiation, *Distant Drum* treats of three themes: the history of India, relationships between men and women, and hunting. Though the history of India becomes a major theme in his later novels, in *Distant Drum* Malgonkar only touches on three historical events in the period from 1938 to 1950: The Burma War in 1941, the New Delhi Riots in September, 1947, and the Indo-Pakistan War over Kashmir in 1949. I shall discuss Malgonkar's treatment of relationships between men and women in the final section of this chapter.

Hunting, as the table of themes shows, is an important theme of *Combat of Shadows* and *The Princes* but completely disappears from *A Bend in the Ganges* and *The Devil's Wind*. In *Distant Drum*, however, there are a few brief references to hunting. Raniwada is described as "ideal fox-hunting country": "Within a few hours you could reach some of the best tiger shooting blocks in Central India, and in winter, the duck, partridge and sandgrouse shooting was as good as any you could get outside a Maharaja's preserve" (34).

Major Harwood, we are told, died as a result of a shikar accident; he died as he went out "to finish off his own tiger" (65). These two passages remind us of the elder Maharaja episode in *The Princes* where the subject of hunting is treated in great detail. Another reference to hunting concerns Kiran himself. He remembers being detailed to shoot an elephant, a tame elephant. Shooting a tame elephant made him feel "shamefully dehumanized" (143). Elephant-shooting has an important place in *Combat of Shadows*. Even the conversation of their officers is seasoned with phrases drawn from the language of hunters — they talk of "finishing off their own tigers." Kiran told Mr. Sonal, for instance, that they always finish off their own tigers (193). The Satpuras, the men of the Fighting Tigers, always repeat the words of Bull Hampton when drinking toasts: "Tigers don't live forever!" (130). "Tigers" also have an important place in *The Princes*.

What is important to stress here is that Malgonkar gives the impression in this first novel of an explorer of his own reservoir of personal experience, his experience both as a Lieutenant Colonel in the British Indian Army and as a professional big-game hunter, making forays into it, but not sure where he should take up position or which segment of experience he should exploit for his fiction or what he should report back. He is feeling his way in a new job as a writer of fiction. As he said in my interview with him:

"I feel that having started writing more or less at a mature age, I don't have to do much research about life because I fall back on experience, you know about army life, about shooting and hunting and the jungle life and some aspects of politics and all that I have gone through. I have experienced them myself. So to that extent it has given me some sort of capital to draw on."

Malgonkar was forty-seven years old when *Distant Drum* was published. Though we do not have here an expertise of craftsmanship, a firm design, penetrating characterization, or a full articulation of a vision that we find in his later fiction, we can still recognize a memorable evocation of Indian Army life and an exploration of relationships between the Britishers and Indians. It is in a sense the epitome of all that is to come.

## II  Combat of Shadows (1962)

The center and core of the book is the story of Henry Winton, a British tea-estate manager in the farthest reaches of the Assam highlands. It is a story which has two stages. The first part, "Prelude to Home Leave," tells of the establishing of relationships between Winton and the Indians and Anglo-Indians. This section also deals with Winton's special relationship with Ruby Miranda. Another episode that brings Britishers and Indians together, revealing their fears and prejudices, is the hunting of the one-tusked elephant. The second part is primarily concerned with Winton's conduct of personal relationships and especially with the dark places in the human heart which make for unhappiness and confusion not only among individuals but also among races and nations. In this part is revealed Winton's moral degeneration culminating in his lonely death in the game cottage, abandoned by Britishers, Indians, and Anglo-Indians.

Henry Winton is a Junior Manager of Silent Hill, a tea garden complete with a factory of the Brindian Tea Company. Somewhat cutoff from the world, Silent Hill is forty-two miles from Chinnar, the headquarters of the tea district where the Resident Directors of the tea companies live. British officers often go to Chinnar because the center of Chinnar is the Highland Club, part hotel, part sports club, a place for the normal relaxations of an English way of life — boating, trout fishing, cricket, golf, tennis, squash, clay-pigeon shooting, dancing. Winton, nearly thirty years old, has put in five years of service and is still an eligible bachelor. He has begun to like his way of life and has become used to the Highland Club, accepting its values without question and sharing its taboos. He would not have given up his life-style for anything else in the world.

At the Brindian Tea Company Winton's immediate boss is Captain Cockburn, the Senior Manager. Sir Jeffrey Dart, the Resident Director at Chinnar, is the highest ranking tea man in the district. Sir Jeffrey and Lady Dart invite Winton to spend an evening with them during the Chinnar Week. On their way to Chinnar Cockburn and Winton stop at Tinapur because the road was blocked by a landslide. At the Railway Institute at Tinapur they attend a gala night where they meet Ruby Miranda, an attractive Anglo-Indian girl. Winton is struck by her "lush, overflowing loveliness" (18). Cockburn suggests that Winton should hire her for his tea garden and make her his mistress "to stop you from going crazy in that antiseptic bungalow of yours" (19).

Cockburn and Winton proceed to Chinnar where Sir Jeffrey and Lady Dart introduce Winton to Miss Jean Walters, daughter of Colonel and Mrs. Walters. Winton admires the "slender and golden-limbed, long-legged, cherry-lipped, blue-eyed and golden-haired" beauty (40). At Sir Jeffrey Dart's home Barloe, the district Commissioner asks Winton to take on the one-tusked Tista, a rogue elephant which had killed four villagers. Winton had shot four elephants before and was considered a good hunter. From this point on Ruby, Jean, and the elephant play a vital role in the life of Henry Winton in his downward drift toward moral degeneration.

Henry falls in love with Jean Walters who often takes the initiative and encourages him to love her. They spend evenings together — even a night — in the game cottage, talking in whispers and clutching each other's hand tightly.

"Would you like to kiss me?"
"Ye-ess"
"Why don't you?" . . .

Henry kissed her. He had known what to expect, and yet it had made him gasp. He felt almost embarrassed by its lingering, searching intimacy. And then he had realized that a woman did not put so much of herself into a kiss unless she was inviting you to go further. He leaned over, forcing her shoulders back. (63)

And yet Jean turns down Henry's proposal of marriage a few weeks later. This disappointment makes Henry turn to Ruby Miranda. He offers her a job in Silent Hill School to bring her closer to him. He makes her the head teacher superseding Sarkar, his present schoolteacher, who had matriculated at Calcutta University. Ruby herself had received very little schooling. Her appointment brought protest from Jugal Kishore, the labor leader.

When Ruby arrives in Silent Hill Henry finds it difficult to keep his thoughts away from her, dreams of her physical charms, and looks forward to the nearness of her body. He longs for her, picturing her "coming into his bungalow in the evenings, ultimately setting up a beautiful dual relationship like that of a fictional French mistress: the perfect, efficient school mistress during office hours, the deliciously wanton companion of non-duty hours" (76).

Ruby begins to come to the bungalow soon after dinner, slipping through the pantry entrance. Henry had set up a campbed for her in the gun room; the only room in the house that could be cut off from the world by closing just one door and sliding a bolt into place. They spend many nights together in this room made for privacy.

District Commissioner Barloe's telegram that the one-tusked rogue elephant had shown up again forces Henry to make plans to set out with his shikari, or tracker, Kistulal. He was embarking on a heady adventure such as comes to a hunter but once in a lifetime. The famed one-tusker had become something of a god to the villagers though it was known to be diabolically cunning and revengeful. Kistulal, the shikari, had no pity for the animals; he was proud of his profession. Unlike the villagers, he was not afraid of the elephant god. It was his business to track an animal down and to get his hunter within range of a shot. He had been a shikari all his conscious life and understood the jungle better than anyone else. Henry calls Kistulal "by far the best tracker in Assam. . . . This fellow's already lame, one leg mauled by a bear; but he's still the best damned tracker in the province" (69).

Henry and Kistulal set out at crack of dawn. The elephant's tracks were already over a day old, and so they did not follow its tracks but decided to move merely in the direction of the tracks. Henry carries his favorite gun, his four-sixty-five double barreled gun and a box of twenty cartridges; Kistulal carries no gun. Late in the afternoon they reach a paddy field and wait for the elephant.

All of a sudden a change comes over Kistulal's face; his perpetual grin disappears. The elephant had come unhesitatingly into the field, huge and gray, wiggling the end of its trunk. Then it located the human scent and charged. Henry, though nervous, raises his rifle, aiming it at the root of the uplifted trunk, and presses the trigger but hears nothing but the cold snap of the hammer pin instead of the roar of the shell going off. He presses the trigger a second time and hears another dead click. He remembered later loading two more cartridges with the elephant barely twenty yards away. They, too, did not work. He ran wildly with panic in his heart. Kistulal in the meanwhile was crushed to death, stamped into the ground in a mess of mud and blood.

After walking miles and miles Henry reached Cockburn's bungalow, wet, disheveled, numb with cold and fear. Cockburn gives him some hot grog and puts him to bed. Next morning Cockburn sent one of his servants to collect the dud cartridges that were dropped in the paddy field. Cockburn advises Henry to make up a story rather than tell the truth.

"Well, it won't do you a bit of good as a hunter; and it won't do you any good as a man — a career man. They'll always say damaging things; they'll even say you got scared at the last moment and ran away. Even the most sympathetic will always say that you were careless in not testing your cartridges before you went out shooting an elephant; a known rogue — a killer . . ." (88 - 89)

The servant brought back only one of the two dud cartridges; he could not find the other in the mangled mess of flesh and blood. Cockburn and Henry agree to make up the following story: Henry was not at the scene of the accident but two hundred yards away from the edge of the field. Kistulal crossed the field where the elephant caught him and killed him. Henry only managed to wound the elephant with one of the cartridges. He did not follow him up and finish him off because he wanted to report his shikari's death. He missed his way coming back in the dark.

Everybody believes Henry's story but Henry himself is worried about the evidence of the missing cartridge. He finds himself often in the grip of a heady depression. Ruby Miranda visits him secretly at night and makes him happy with her "flawless olive skin and contours of the harem favourite" (97). During one of her visits Ruby tells Henry of her involvement with Eddie Trevor. Eddie is in love with her and wants to marry her as soon as he gets a job.

Eddie had obtained the job of chief stockman when Jugal Kishore resigned. His appointment led to a wave of protest from labor leaders who serve a formal notice of their intention to strike. Eddie, Henry's rival for Ruby's favors, has also become the cause of a threatened strike. The strikers keep shouting:

"We want!
Jus-tice!
Mister Trevor!
Never, never!
Winton Sahib!
Chale Jao" (137)

Henry handled the tricky situation with tact and understanding; the workers returned to work because they were afraid of the police firing. Henry no doubt averted the strike, but the crisis makes him ask for home leave immediately.

At the beginning of Part II, "Return From Home Leave," Henry returns from England after eight months of leave. He is married to Jean Walters. At the Silent Hill he begins to rearrange his life. He wants to get rid of Ruby Miranda, who now hates him with an all-consuming bitterness. She had tried terribly hard to catch the Englishman. Ruby is given the job of a housekeeper at the Highland Club. She was planning to get married to Eddie Trevor, who was recommended for a commission in the Army by Sir Jeffrey. Eddie's engagement is to be announced before he goes up for his training.

Eddie and Jean had traveled in the same boat once. They had even danced and won a competition together. At Silent Hill they renew their friendship and friendship gradually turns into sexual passion. They meet each other secretly and spend hours together as lovers. Bitterness and anger rise within Henry when Gauri points out Eddie and Jean at Wallach's Folly, lying side by side on a small blue rug spread under the branches of a tree.

He could not bear to see what he saw, and yet he went on looking as if spellbound; just as he had gone on looking at the elephant trampling down Kistulal. And what he saw now was far more horrible than the death of his shikari. . . . He felt a sudden, nervous shiver run down his body. (252)

Henry wants to shoot them on the spot but couldn't do it with his rifle. He could do it if he had the .265 Mauser handy.

At this time the elephant, the one-tusker that had killed Kistulal, was reported to be in the valley. The elephant had come right into the

Koyna valley, which Henry could overlook from his bungalow. It had come all the way from Lamlung, thirty miles away and had taken nearly a year to cover the distance. Henry is once again asked to go after the rogue elephant even though he doesn't like to do so now, a year after the accident. Oscillating between extremes of confidence and despair he prepares himself for the hunting trip — tests a box of fresh cartridges, checks his rifle. He goes alone with his rifle and binoculars into the impenetrable jungle in search of the elephant for days, but he does not see it; he sees only its droppings and the evidence of its lordly passage through the bamboos and reeds. On the day he finally locates it, he has an accident at Wallach's Folly and twists his ankle, and therefore can not walk to the jungle to shoot the elephant.

Eddie Trevor wants to finish the job. He asks Henry to lend him his four-sixty-five and cartridges. Henry is perfectly willing to let Eddie shoot the one-tusker.

". . . Look, if you really do want to go, I wouldn't mind letting you have my rifle and telling you exactly where he's going to be."

"Oh, Mr. Winton! I shall be most grateful. Yes, I really do want to go. . . ." (260)

Henry plans Eddie's murder carefully. The cards were falling just right. He gives Eddie his big elephant gun and a box of cartridges — the very box from which the faulty cartridges were taken earlier. The murder is foolproof. Eddie goes out hunting with Pasupati and never comes back. He is killed by the elephant, his body trampled and broken and gored. Sir Jeffrey later kills the one-tusker with his own gun and cartridges.

Henry is left alone; Jean leaves him to live with her aunt at Poona. The Army does not accept him because of his broken ankle. Ruby Miranda once again becomes Henry's obsession. He wants to marry her, not simply to keep her as a mistress. When Sir Jeffrey asks Henry to go up to the game cottage and find out what is wrong with its artificial moon, he thinks of the visit as an opportunity to invite Ruby Miranda to the game cottage for a reunion. That is where he would ask her to be his wife.

Pasupati helped him to climb up the steps of the cottage. Henry asked him to go to Miranda and bring back dinner for two. It was pitch dark. The artificial moon blinks on and off for several seconds before it comes on. Something was terribly wrong with it. Henry lies down after switching the moon off and waits for Ruby Miranda and dinner.

Hours later the forest was on fire. A cold fear runs through him when he discovers that even the ladder to climb down is gone. Someone pulls out a fuse from the electric box and the artificial moon goes out. There was a basket at the end of a rope. He pulls it up and peers into it. It contains the shell of his four-sixty-five rifle and the sapphire and gold ear clips he had given Ruby Miranda. "And that . . . was the moment of truth . . . the smell of parrafin was strong in his nostrils, and the flames were leaping all about him" (289). Sir Jeffrey, Ruby Miranda, and Pasupati had planned Henry's murder perfectly just as he had planned Eddie's earlier.

Clearly, the two dominant themes of *Combat of Shadows* are Indo-British relationships at the personal level and hunting. As in *Distant Drum* Malgonkar continues to explore the relationships between British managers and the Indians and Anglo-Indians they control. There is, however, an important difference between the two novels. In *Distant Drum* Malgonkar treats British officers with sympathy; all of them appear to be courtly gentlemen. In *Combat of Shadows* the Britishers are not admirable but corrupt and immoral; Henry Winton, Cockburn, Jean Walters, and Sir Jeffrey Dart, and others are hated by Indians and Anglo-Indians. Malgonkar concentrates on the darker side of the nature of the ruling Britisher rather than the brighter side, as he does in *Distant Drum*. The second theme — hunting — is dealt with in great detail in *Combat of Shadows*. It was only briefly touched on in *Distant Drum*, as we have seen.

A glance at the Table of Themes reveals another point about the evolution of the novelist. "Indo-British relationships at the personal level, Malgonkar's No. 1 theme in *Distant Drum* and *Combat of Shadows*, becomes a less important minor theme in his later fiction. (No. 5 in *The Princes*, No. 4 in *A Bend in the Ganges* and *The Devil's Wind*). It is clear that he turns to other themes — the history of India and initiation — in his later novels for detailed treatment. It is these two themes that provide continuity among his works. What is true of Indo-British relationships is also true of the theme of hunting. He touches briefly on hunting in *Distant Drum*, as we have seen. In *Combat of Shadows*, however, hunting is a dominant theme — most characters are seen in terms of their reactions to the shooting of the elephant. Henry Winton makes love in the game cottage and dies in the game cottage. The theme of hunting, however, disappears from his later fiction — *A Bend in the Ganges* and *The Devil's Wind*. In *The Princes* it is No. 4. Malgonkar does not deal with the themes of the history of India and initiation in *Combat of Shadows*. There are only brief references to the elections in Assam in 1939 and to the Second World War. Malgonkar also does not show Henry growing up before us; we see him growing more and more morally corrupt.

Indo-British relationships and hunting are intertwined in *Combat of Shadows*. Henry has to pretend to be a good hunter before Indians and Anglo-Indians and not let his side down. Sir Jeffrey warns him on one occasion: "Remember that the Empire is a hellish big thing, but in the last analysis it is nothing more than a few thousands of hard-core men like you and me doing our jobs and taking care not to let the side down' " (34).

After Kistulal's accidental death Cockburn advises Henry not to worry about the moral obligations of a hunter toward his Indian shikari. The important thing is to present the image of a great and successful hunter; to confess failure before Indians is to let the side down. Cockburn says:

"It will kill your reputation as a big game hunter. . . . Sudden will never forgive you for having let down the side . . . the Indian ministers will laugh their heads off; and the villagers will whisper behind your back, pointing a finger at you . . . this incident now will make all the difference between success and failure. If you are determined to make a go of your career here, you cannot afford to be tied down to a suburban conscience. . . ." (89 - 90)

This is the beginning of Henry's corruption — he goes ahead, suppresses the evidence of the faulty cartridges and lets people believe that Kistulal, his expert tracker, foolishly allowed himself to be trampled by the rogue elephant. As a matter of fact Kistulal had done his job; Henry had not done his due to the dud cartridges he had taken with him without testing beforehand. This episode of Henry's cowardice and corruption reminds us of George Orwell's celebrated essay on "Shooting an Elephant" (1936)[1] in which "the real nature of imperialism — the real motives for which despotic governments act" is discussed. Orwell, as Subdivisional Police officer, was asked to kill a rogue elephant ravaging a bazaar; he marches down the hill toward the paddy fields with a large crowd following him. The elephant was only eight yards from the road but Orwell does not want in the least to kill him. But the crowd of two thousand was watching him and did not allow him to go without shooting the elephant. Orwell says:

And suddenly I realized that I should have to shoot the elephant after all. The people expected it of me and I had got to do it. . . . And it was at this moment, as I stood there with the rifle in hands, that I first grasped the hollowness, the futility of the white man's dominion in the East. Here was I, the white man with his gun, standing in front of the unarmed native crowd — seemingly the leading actor of the piece; but in reality I was only an absurd puppet pushed to and fro by the will of those yellow faces behind. I perceived in this moment that when the white man turns tyrant it is his own freedom that he destroys. He becomes a sort of hollow, posing dummy . . . Sahib. For it is the condition of his rule that he shall spend his life in trying to impress the "natives," and so in every crisis he has got to do what the "natives" expect of him. . . . I had got to shoot the elephant. . . . To come all that way, rifle in hand, with two thousand people marching at my heels, and then to trail feebly away, having done nothing — no, that was impossible. The crowd would laugh at me. And my whole life, every white man's life in the East was one long struggle not to be laughed at. (158 - 159)

Similar thoughts go through Henry's head: "There was no room in India for Sahibs who failed, that was the over-riding truth; they were despised even more by their class than by the Indians. Failure was unthinkable; it was the abyss, dark and bottomless" (90).

And so the shooting of the one-tusked rogue elephant becomes an extremely complex political and moral event, affecting the relationships of people, in *Combat of Shadows.* It corrupts Henry and Cockburn who do not tell the truth about those cartridges. It leads to two murders — Kistulal's and Eddie Trevor's, the one unplanned but the other planned carefully by Henry. It makes Kistulal's son, Pasupati, extremely suspicious of Henry. It makes even Jugal Kishore, Assam's minister, intervene to keep Henry in Assam and not allow him to join the army. There is even a suggestion that Sir Jeffrey himself begins to distrust Henry after Eddie's death. Facing the flames of the forest in the game cottage Henry wonders about Sir Jeffrey:

And then he found himself sinking into doubt once again, wondering if Sudden too had a hand in this; Sudden who had sent him to inspect the game cottage moon when he must have known that it was a job for an electrician; Sudden who had so studiedly avoided looking him in the eye throughout their interview that morning. (289)

Henry had been haunted by the missing cartridge which was returned to him in the last scene. The four-sixty-five double barreled elephant gun, the cartridges, and above all the one-tusked elephant appear and reappear to influence Henry's personal relationships.

Henry works with people he hates. He is very much like Colonel Manners in *Distant Drum* who hates India and Indians. Henry hates Indians and Anglo-Indians and is hated by them. Jugal Kishore tells him: "Your failing is that you cannot bear Indians; yet your tragedy is that you are doomed to work in this country" (111). Gauri, Jugal Kishore's niece, calls Henry a "White monster" (139). Even Henry's one-time mistress, Ruby Miranda, calls him "brute." "You white swine! I hate you — I hate you!" (152).

All this hate is the result of his own hatred of Indians and Anglo-Indians. At the time of the strike he reveals his feelings toward laborers. He says: " 'that's the only way to deal with coolies. They're like animals. Once they begin their headlong stampede no one can stop them; before the stampede begins, you can whip them back' " (143). His intense hate toward Eddie, Ruby's boyfriend, makes him plan Eddie's murder:

The thought of a man like Eddie Trevor looking upon him as a rival, as another man competing for Ruby Miranda's favours, had brought on a surge of nausea. That was a revolting position. No one should point a finger at him as the rival of a raw, half-caste youth; . . . (127)

After Henry's marriage with Jean Walters Henry continues to lust after Ruby Miranda. And when Ruby refuses him, Henry explodes and reveals his real prejudice against Anglo-Indians: " 'You half-caste slut . . . you don't deserve anything better than your colony and your half-breed lovers . . . speaking your own brand of the English language . . .' " (153). Later Henry's wife, too, dislikes him and leaves him. Malgonkar presents Henry as a throughly corrupt and despicable Britisher with no redeeming qualities.

*Combat of Shadows* contains some of the best descriptions of hunting in the Indian jungles, reminding readers of Hemingway and Corbett. Henry, Kistulal, Eddie, Cockburn, Pasupati, and Dart are all deeply involved in hunting and killing animals. The action is set in Assam,

the expanse of man-high wild grass dotted with carefully preserved clumps of trees where the annual rough-shoot took place — a day-long drive for red jungle cock, chukor, hare, and three kinds of pheasant. . . . You could almost bank on seeing a bison or two, and on a good night deer and wild pig and possibly a leopard or an elephant. . . . (25 - 26)

True, the shooting of the elephant is the central action of the novel and the supreme hunter is Henry. Henry had killed elephants before — three tuskers and one Makna. But there are times when even he is filled with fear and despair and appears to be the hunted rather than the hunter. The rogue elephant seems "determined to seek him out and destroy him, an enemy more hateful than Jugal Kishore himself, a private Hitler" (237 - 38). The elephant comes all the way from Lamlung, about thirty miles, and reappears in the Koyna valley near Henry's bungalow nearly a year after it was first seen. Henry's joys and sorrows as a hunter are described vividly.

A true hunter is not afraid of the thing he wants to kill, nor does he hate it; indeed, in a sense he loves that which he seeks to destroy. What a hunter looks forward to is the chase itself, the matching of wits against an animal of the jungle on its own ground, and then coming face to face with it; not the actual act of killing — the killing nearly always came as an anti-climax . . . Henry knew that he was secretly afraid of the elephant, and hated it because he was afraid. . . . (237)

It is not only the elephant that the hunters go after. Eddie Trevor shoots a python with Henry's gun. The mating call of the pythons — the vibrating, the booming Ooo — is often heard in the Assam valleys.

In writing *Combat of Shadows* Malgonkar found a way to articulate and organize his hunting experience. It is an aspect of his experience that he uses in his fiction only once more — in *The Princes*.

### III   *The Images of Women*

It is time for a long second look at the two early novels together. This is perhaps the place to enlarge upon another theme of Malgonkar's fiction — the theme of relationships between men and women. Specifically, the images of women in his fiction. How are women portrayed in these early novels? Does his treatment of women in the early novels tell us something about women in his later novels? One of the most striking aspects of Malgonkar's fiction is the importance of men. One after the other, from *Distant Drum* (1960) to *The Devil's Wind* (1972), men are the central characters. It is men who are the real focus of these novels — Kiran Garud in *Distant Drum*, Henry Winton in *Combat of Shadows* (1962), Abhay in *The Princes* (1963), Gian Talvar and Debi-dayal in *A Bend in the Ganges* (1964), and Nana Saheb in *The Devil's Wind* (1972). What is a woman's place in this essentially man's world?

Before dealing with portraits of women in Malgonkar's fiction, let me begin with some negations. Malgonkar's novels are *not* social documents; they are autonomous works of fiction. Criticism within the past few decades has repudiated errant speculation about the previous or subsequent history of characters, men or women, and has focused attention on the works themselves free from irrelevancies concerning the author's life, or the life of the characters. We have not forgotten L. C. Knight's famous essay "How Many Children has Lady Macbeth?" which severely condemned all speculative excursions away from the texts themselves. It is important to remind ourselves that a novel is a novel, not something else; it is not a work of sociology or of psychology. Nor is it a report on the status of women in India today. The literary critic must stay within the work itself. Clearly, the study of women in Malgonkar's novels should be approached with a good deal of critical caution. The study of these women may at best offer valuable hints about the prevailing social attitude toward women, and perhaps about the personal attitude of the author himself. We can never be perfectly sure that we have found both. Possibly such a study will merely confirm what we sense already as significant in his method of feminine characterization.

Nor are Malgonkar's novels concerned with a number of specifically feminine problems that shape every woman's life. He maintains an almost complete silence on the following feminine problems: resolving the "Electra" problem; establishing feminine identity including the problem of resolving conflicts with the mother; fluctuations of the menstrual cycle; fears and rewards of childbirth; loss of beauty and menopause; problems related to a woman active in the public sphere; genuine difficulty or joy of mothering; friendship between two women; and power conflicts between two women. All these are serious problems women deal with daily. Yet Malgonkar's novels seldom if ever show them doing so.

Malgonkar's novels give the impression — a false impression when one looks at the primary focus of the novels — that they teem with women. For my purposes here I should like to consider all women that appear in Malgonkar's five novels: *Distant Drum, Combat of Shadows, The Princes, A Bend in the Ganges,* and *The Devil's Wind.* This means that I would like to inspect not only all characters — major and minor — of the narratives themselves, that is, those that make contributions to the action of the novels, but also characters not strictly in the fiction itself but referred to by other characters or by the novelist.

My census of women in these five novels shows a total of fifty-eight. This is not, of course, the total population of women in the novels. I have taken no account of the women at the dances at the Officers' Club *(Distant Drum)* or of the coolie women at the Brindian Tea Company *(Combat of Shadows)* or of the palaces of the Maharajah *(The Princes)* or of the convoy *(A Bend in the Ganges)* or of Bithoor Palace *(The Devil's Wind)*. I have only considered in my total those that are named. My count does not include the nameless women, although we know from the novelist's references that they are there.

Some details of the census may be mentioned here. Based on their defining relationships with men, one may break down the women into three large groups, or, perhaps more accurately, into three stereotyped images of women: submissive wives, sex objects or concubines, and sensual women. While the nuances of their roles vary, their identity remains the same. There are twenty-two submissive wives, ten sex objects or concubines, and six sensual women. Another point that becomes immediately apparent from this census is that there are no heroines or protagonists among these women. Nor are there "round" characters among them; they are all "flat" characters in E. M. Forster's sense of the term. They are constructed round a single idea or quality and they possess nothing of the incalculability or unpredictability of life of the "round" characters. One might almost suspect that Malgonkar did not choose to endow his women with flesh and blood, with complex and ambigious natures but rather emphasized one aspect of character while leaving out others of equal or greater importance. This is what makes his feminine characters appear to be stereotypes. The flattering frequency with which these fifty-eight women appear and reappear in these five novels is rather deluding; they appear not as they are but largely as conveniences for the resolution of the masculine problems of heroes around whom the novels are centered — Kiran, Henry, Abhay, Gian, Debi-dayal, and Nana. Women are often seen as subsidiary parts of essentially masculine problems.

This brief glance at the census suggests another point. There are four other stereotypes of women very much noticeable in Western literature that Malgonkar has not dealt with. Perhaps this tells us very little about the women themselves; but it can tell us something about his method of feminine characterization. One will search in vain in his novels for the following four stereotypes. First, the dominating wife. Destructive, castrating, and assertive women like

Martha in *Who's Afraid of Virginia Woolf?* Second, the sentimental woman — emotional, irrational, hysterical, and helpless. Third, the "liberated" woman — educated, self-actualizing, independent, confident, and committed to career, the woman with a "room of her own" and a comfortable income. And fourth, the single woman or old maid — unattractive, unhappy, unwanted, and sterile.

Let us now turn to Malgonkar's literary treatment of the three stereotypes that appear and reappear virtually unchanged in the novels. The submissive wives of one novel are not different from the submissive wives of another. If the sex objects or concubines of one novel were put in another, not much would be altered. And the sensual women, too, are alike. Clearly, these are in a sense "heroines" with a thousand faces. All fifty-eight women are condemned to variations of the three stereotypes.

## A.  *Submissive Wives*

She is easy to spot. She is angel in the house, the homemaker, the nourisher and fosterer of life, the heart of family life, the source of tender loving care. She may appear retiring and submissive in the public but in private life she is responsible in her roles as wife, mother, daughter-in-law, and finally as mother-in-law for the solidarity of the family and the continuation of its values. She is a civilizing and humanizing influence on men. She may not be an ecstatic housewife like the housewives of the fairy-tale land of American TV commercials, always proud of the sparkle of dishes and the dazzle of linen, but she goes about her domestic duties reasonably calmly and finds deep fulfillment in the care and feeding of human beings, the cementing of meaningful relationships, service, and love. Unlike her American sister, she has high self-esteem and knows nothing of her self-hatred. She seems to be aware of her unique sexual identity and her traditional avenue to happiness. To the Western woman she might appear like a household drudge with 140-hour week, no retirement, no sick leave, no room of her own, and no Sundays off! She, however, is not suffering from any "problem that has no name"; she is not desperately trying to live up to the media image of the model woman. Her private image is not built on magazine and television commercials.

Leela, Arun's wife in *Distant Drum,* and Kamala, Abhay's wife chosen from two photographs, in *The Princes* are two examples of this stereotype. Both of them appear briefly in the novels but their presence is not forgotten even if they quickly withdraw into the kitchen or behind the curtains. Leela is introduced as "friendly, full of life, always natural, immune to Arun's overpowering moods" (8). She does not take part in the discussion with her husband and his friends, though she smiles and walks briskly among them. After the drinks she took Bina to the train station. " 'Don't let them run away," ' Leela called out from the car. " 'I have ordered a nice dinner' " (11). And then she disappears from the scene and from the novel. We don't read more about her in the novel.

Kamala, also, appears only in a few pages and then drops out of the novel, though we know she bore children for Abhay. Abhay gave his consent to marry her by letter without even asking to see another photograph or to see the girl. As for the girl herself we know absolutely nothing of her feelings or thoughts about the marriage. Perhaps she did not even have a photograph of Abhay. It was a conventional Hindu arranged marriage brought about by the pundits matching horoscopes. But the marriage turned out to be a happy one: "mine is certainly not an unusual example of how love can flow as a consequence of marriage, living together and the begetting of children . . ." (220).

Other wives home-oriented and willing to submerge their identities when they marry in these novels may be mentioned: Mrs. Kotwal, Mrs. Kagal, Mrs. Travers *(Distant Drum);* Mrs. Miranda, Mrs. Dart, Mrs. Trevor, Mrs. Walters *(Combat of Shadows);* Mrs. Hinks *(The Princes);* Debi's mother, Basu's wife, Aji, Mulligan's wife *(A Bend in the Ganges);* Nana's first wife; second wife, Girija; third wife, Kashi; Mrs. Wheeler; and Mrs. Hillersdon *(The Devil's Wind).* It is interesting to note that even their names are not given; only their relationship with men is indicated. They are all their *husbands'* wives.

## B.  *Sex Objects or Concubines*

A sex object is defined as an object because such a woman is here reduced to a thing. A man cares about her only in so far as she serves him. She is regarded as only a body; there is no suggestion that she is a person. She is presented simply as a pleasure-giving commodity. The following words often describe these women: "luscious," "peach," "filly," and "wench" in *Combat of Shadows* (14, 17, 238, 531, 30, 9). She sells sex, not love. Sometimes she herself is bought and sold. For example, Mumtaz in *A Bend in the Ganges* says that her uncle sold her when she was eleven years old. Azurie, another mistress in the same novel, was sold for eight thousand rupees even though she had already had two babies. Cockburn in *Combat of Shadows* gives a bit of advice to Henry about women — to treat them simply as sex objects: " 'You keep to the coolie women, and you'll never have any problems on your hands. . . . Terrific value for money, and no complications; safe as houses. Have your fun by all means . . .' " (22). On another occasion Cockburn, speaking coldly, puts a price tag on these women:

" . . . There's no morality involved. . . . The moment you get browned off, you pack them off; give them a little money, fifty chips or so, and everything is tickety-boo. . . . And even if you do give them a brat, there's nothing to worry about, really. Couple of hundred chips, and they'll find a proud father." (14)

Sir Jeffrey Dart himself had fathered Eddie Trevor whose mother was Sir Jeffrey's mistress. Ruby Miranda is a sex object or mistress for Henry only for a short time before his marriage. Henry tries his best to make Ruby his mistress even after his marriage, but Ruby refuses to cooperate after she recognizes that she is only a sex object for Henry. She regards him as a "man of lust without love, who was merely seeking physical fulfillment and paying her a hundred rupees a month of the company's money for his private pleasure . . ." (101). Like all bachelor planters Henry, too, has to have a mistress. "They had to have them, sometimes two or three at a time, mainly from among the coolie women, of course. . . . You couldn't live in the jungle for three-year terms between home leaves without something like that to keep you sane. . . ." (154).

Malgonkar's discussion of the mistresses in these novels is virtually always limited to physical aspects of their relationships with men as if they were the only relationships that these women have thus their relationsips with other women, with children, and wi' society in general are significantly diminished. Sherawathi in *Th Princes* is described as "the one woman I have seen who gave the in pression of being absolutely naked even when fully clothed; sensuou and slim, supple, dark and shining like a black cobra swaying" (56) Bibi-bai, another mistress in *The Princes,* is "earthy and raw-boned, and to me she always looked unwashed with her hair straying all over her face." Nana's mistress Azijan in *The Devil's Wind* is described as follows: "In the sunlight her bared shoulders shone like oiled teak . . . her breasts which were the same color as her shoulders, not lighter as in most women, were set well apart and had the classical mango shape so that the reddened nipples pointed outwards . . ." (30 - 31).

## C.   *Sensual Women*

The sensual woman is defined as sensual because she arouses in men the most uncontrollable passions and makes them tend toward "sinful" behavior. She is provocatively sexy without being a sex object. She is sexually aggressive, single or married, very disruptive, and in Malgonkar's novels she is generally a fair, Westernized, Eurasian, or white woman. This last point is worth stressing — Malgonkar's sensual women are either Eurasian or Western women, not Indian women. These sensual women are sexually insatiable, sleep around a good deal, and yet seem to be in control of their own sexuality, using it for their purposes rather than being used by it. They passionately pursue pleasures of the senses particularly those associated with sexual pleasure regardless of consequences. The word that Malgonkar uses often to describe their essential nature is "wanton." "Margot . . . warm, perfumed and naked and deliciously wanton . . ." (93). Ruby is "the perfect, efficient school mistress during office hours, the deliciously wanton companion of non-duty hours" (76). She had been "docile as a chinese concubine, so deliciously wanton in the privacy of the bungalow . . ." (153 - 54). Minnie's "slim, bold, deliciously wanton" (227).

There are only a few portraits of sensual women in his novels — Margot Medley *(Distant Drum),* Ruby Miranda, and Jean Walters *(Combat of Shadows);* Minnie Bradley *(The Princes);* Sylvia Bolten, Mrs. Scobie, and Eliza Wheeler *(The Devil's Wind).*

Margot Medley, the wife of Major Medley, did a lot of things with a great deal of zest and a lot else which, if you were callously outspoken, you could call exhibitionism . . . Her chief asset was a pair of attractive legs which she was always careful to display to full advantage. . . . She would keep wriggling her legs all the time. . . . (19)

In sexual matters Margot is often the aggressor. She throws herself at men (5). It is she who takes the initiative. It was one of her legs that had come from under the bamboo table, reaching out like a snake, to play games with Kiran's bare ankle, and sent a delightful, electric thrill through him" (20). It is she who invites Kiran to her flat in Calcutta to spend a night with her (24 - 27). Though married she has clandestine affairs with Kiran, Abdul Jamal, and an American Air Corps Major.

Ruby Miranda "had bold roving eyes of a Chandni-Chowk whore and the full-blown contours of a harem favorite." (19). As we have seen she refuses to be Henry's mistress or sex object — after his marriage with Jean Walters. She is presented as essentially a sensual woman. Henry's thoughts often turn to her "heavy-bosomed and narrow-hipped — the thought of her body so temptingly close at hand sent a delicious thrill through him (97). . . . At times, Ruby had found herself trembling with fear but also trembling even more with desire." (102). She loves both Eddie and Henry passionately but hates Henry when he marries Jean Walters. She had often gone to Henry's bungalow at nights to be in his bed, "on the white sheets naked and desirable and desiring, her hands folded behind her head and smiling at him with half-closed eyes in token of her surrender" (117).

Jean Walters, too, is a sensual woman, "deceptively demure on the surface, delightfully volatile underneath" (49). She does not mind the light when making love. Hers was a "wilder, less restrained, even more aggressive, more demanding, more exhausting kind of love-making — not the kind which throve only in darkness. Even to think of it sent a delightful tingle through his body" (169). Jean is sexually aggressive. When she and Henry were strolling on the moonlit lawn one night he attempts to kiss her.

It was a hesitant, even half-hearted sort of kiss when it began, but Jean had taken it over from him and transformed it into a lingering, searing moment of bliss; starting from nowhere, it had become an exploration into forbidden territory, a kiss of hunger and thirst and desire. . . . (47)

It is Jean who asks Henry to kiss her: "Would you like to kiss me? . . . Why don't you?" (61). After marriage it is again she who takes the initiative: " 'Take me in your arms,' she ordered, putting her own arms tightly around his neck. 'Lift me up. I am the bride. . . .' " (171). Later she is unfaithful and takes Eddie Trevor as her lover, and when Eddie dies Jean leaves her husband without hesitation.

These sensual women exhibit more of the "freedom and gaiety of the West" than the "submissiveness and surrender of the oriental womanhood" (*Combat of Shadows,* 116). They are often contrasted with the submissive wives at the other end of the scale. Kamala in *The Princes* is described as follows: "But I had not married her for love; she was not capable of causing any great emotional stir within me, even though she could be the subject of a purely proprietary pride" (239). But Minnie is not like her: "She was somehow part of the morning, of the verve and vitality of spring, volatile and blooming . . . fresh as a morning dew" (131). Later Abhay compares her to a Hindu wife: "I was thinking of Minnie, comparing her, lively and gay and bold, to a Hindu girl who would not raise her eyes to see what her husband looked like" (164).

What is the significance of these stereotypes? We scarcely have space here to discuss their implications; however, we can make a few tentative comments. If one grants the assumption that fiction is a valid index of how people think and feel and act — many literary critics will not grant this assumption — Malgonkar's fiction does not give woman a place of importance. As has been pointed out, his novels define women essentially as submissive wives, sex objects, and sensual persons. Readers of his novels might say: "Maybe it's not fair, but that's how it is. It is a man's world. They are a man's novels. Men *are* more important in society because they *do,* in fact, hold the principal roles which govern it."

The trouble with this rather tidy explanation, however, is that it doesn't really explain things. In India women *are* important — the Prime Minister of India is a woman and many others hold positions of importance. Major social and economic changes are taking place in India which are contributing to changing and improving men's concept of women and women's self-concept. The successful women in India are giving women a new image of what they could be and of their potentialities, and Indian society is encouraging women to fulfill their potentialities as human beings at home as well as outside the home. Women are revising their values, reorganizing their homes, and reentering the world. They are making considered and careful choices from among a great many alternatives. Several subtle and largely traditional cultural preconceptions about the role of women in India are vanishing, and women are developing a self-concept which is foreign to their traditional role. But Malgonkar has failed to capture this body of feminine experience in India in all its ambiguity and complexity and diversity. His women are not drawn in depth and detail. He has failed to challenge the supremacy of the stereotype. His are women — not as they are, but as *he wished they were.* In his novels there is not a single woman as protagonist who is self-actualizing and independent but also capable of loving and being loved.

To sum up then: when we examine Malgonkar's two early novels and three later novels together we see five chief strands — themes — binding them together. We must remember that extracting these five themes is necessarily an act of oversimplification; it is only through their complex relationships with subsidiary motifs and with straightforward narration that they help us to identify the novelist's evolution or progress. Even though his early novels are not his best works, properly read, they can tell us a great deal about the important and continuous themes of all his fiction, his "vision" of life. In manner and theme they contain all his later fiction. True, his portraits of Englishmen in the early novels are not convincing enough; they have simple surfaces, no depths. Nor is the initiation theme fully developed. Indian history is not yet a major theme; it is merely the background, not the very stuff of his novels as in his later novels. Nevertheless, we can see within the course of less than a decade the themes of initiation and the history of India emerge from comparative unimportance to become the focus of his later novels. Malgonkar has come a long way in a short time to become one of the best Indian novelists in English.

## CHAPTER 3

# The Historian of the Marathas:
# Kanhoji Angrey, Puars of Dewas
# Senior, *and* Chhatrapatis of Kolhapur

M ALGONKAR'S three books of history — *Kanhoji Angrey* (1959), *Puars of Dewas Senior* (1963), and *Chhatrapatis of Kolhapur* (1971) — deal with the rise and fall of the Marathas. Between Chhatrapati Shivaji (1627 - 1680), the founder of the Maratha Empire and Chhatrapati Shahaji Maharaj, the present Chhatrapati of Kolhapur, lie three centuries of history and a world of faded dreams. During the seventeenth and eighteenth centuries the Marathas challenged the Moghuls and the British alike for supremacy over the whole of India. The once-powerful Maratha Empire was the principal power that the British overthrew to gain control over the entire subcontinent. Between 1775 and 1818 the British fought three wars — in 1775, 1803, and 1817 — that finally shattered the Maratha Confederation and led to full British Supremacy.

The term Maratha (Mahratta, Mahrathi) is used to denote the kingdom founded by the Maratha leader Shivaji in the seventeenth century and expanded to the status of an empire by his successors in the eighteenth century. The term is also used, often loosely, to designate the entire regional population speaking the Marathi language. The Marathi-speaking region of Peninsular India extends eastward from the Goa, Bombay, and Thana districts on the Arabian Sea 800 miles east of Nagpur. Malgonkar's three books of history focus attention on Maratha leaders of three areas: Kanhoji Angrey, the lord of Konkan, a thin sliver of west coast of India beginning at Bassein in the north and ending at Karwar in the south; Puars of Dewas Senior, rulers of a small princely state in the middle of India of about 446 square miles with a population of 80,000; and Chhatrapatis of Kolhapur, rulers of another larger princely state, hundreds of miles south of Dewas Senior.

Malgonkar's mother-tongue is Marathi. He lives in a Marathi-speaking area and concentrates in his historical writings on Maratha

history. I asked him why he focuses on Maratha history rather than
Indian history. He said:

"There are two answers to this question, both connected. First, Indian
history is so vast. You know, you can begin from almost 5th century B.C. So
one has to specialize. You can't say I will delve into all Indian history,
because even you would not even be able to read the books in your lifetime
about that time in history. One can only get a background. So I believe the
second and connected answer to your question is that I like to know my
history, to read my history as far as possible in the original and there are a
great many documents in Marathi on the Maratha history, which has confined my territory to Maratha history. And then again, I don't consider
myself to be a student of the entire Maratha history. I just perhaps have
chosen a corner, a small area of Maratha history itself."[1]

Shivaji (Sivaji Bhonsla, 1627 - 1680), the founder of the Maratha
Kingdom, was the son of Shahji Bhonsla, who was in the service of
the Muslim Kingdom of Bijapur. Fearless and adored, Shivaji turned
against Bijapur and Mughal rulers after his father's death. He
plundered their territories with his small Maratha army and in 1674
crowned himself at Raigarh as an independent sovereign or
Chhatrapati (*Chhatra* — "umbrella" or "canopy," *pati* — "master"
or "captain"). From 1674 to 1680 he worked tirelessly and laid the
foundations of a compact and independent kingdom in Western India.

Kanhoji Angrey (1669 - 1729) the Maratha Admiral, called the
"pirate" by the English, dominated the west coast between Bombay
and Goa in the first years of the eighteenth century. Malgonkar's
*Kanhoji Angrey Maratha Admiral: An Account of his Life and his
Battles With the English* (1959) deals not only with the achievements
of this brilliant Maratha naval commander but also with his relations
with Shivaji's successors — Sambhaji (1680 - 87), Rajaram (1689-
1760), and Tarabai (1700 - 1708). Malgonkar calls this book of
history "an historical biography."

When Shivaji Chhatrapati died at Raigarh on April 3, 1680, he left
two sons, born of different mothers, as successors — Sambhaji and
Rajaram. Sambhaji was twenty-two years old, Rajaram ten.
Sambhaji succeeded Shivaji but was executed by the Mughal
Emperor in 1687. Rajaram was proclaimed Regent in February,
1687, but was whisked off to a fort called Jinji for protection.
Disputes arose over the claim for the kingdom founded by

Chhatrapati Shivaji between the descendants of Sambhaji and Rajaram. The former reigned over the Satara Branch and the latter became the founders of the Kolhapur Branch. Malgonkar's *Chhatrapatis of Kolhapur* is a history of this Kolhapur branch of the House of Shivaji — a branch very much neglected by historians who have been preoccupied with the Satara Branch. At Poona power passed in the eighteenth century to a line of Brahmins serving as Peshwa (Prime ministers). During the decline of Maratha fortunes the office of the Peshwa became hereditary and the line ended in Nana Sahib, one of the leaders of the Indian Mutiny of 1857. Nana is the protagonist of Malgonkar's *The Devil's Wind.*

*Puars of Dewas Senior* is also a contribution to the history of the Marathas. The kingdom of Dewas was founded by two Maratha brothers who came into Malwa with Baji Rao in 1728. E. M. Forster visited Dewas Senior in 1912 - 13 and in 1921 and wrote about its Maharaja Sir Tukoji Rao III and his son Vikramsinharao in *The Hill of Devi* (1953). Maharaja Vikramsinharao Puar, the heir apparent to the Maharaja of Dewas Senior, became the ruler of Kolhapur state as Chhatrapati Shahaji Maharaj in 1947. Since independence Dewas Senior was merged in Madhya Bharat on June 27, 1948, and Madhya Bharat became part of Madhya Pradesh state on November 1, 1956. Kolhapur state, too, was merged in Bombay state on March 1, 1949. All the princely states lost their identity after independence.

To attempt to summarize these three books of history, covering over three hundred years in 1200 pages, dealing with details of the life of kings and their battles, would be to falsify history. Therefore, what I have done instead is to point out some salient features of these historical works, and to evaluate Malgonkar as a professional historian. His achievement as a historical novelist is discussed elsewhere. Appendix 1, *Historical Chronology,* see page 157, lists the major events of the Maratha history.

## I  *Kanhoji Angrey*

Indian history books call Kanhoji "the warden of the West Coast." His whole military career is often handled in a sentence or two. Historians pay little attention to this extraordinary man who ruled the waters of the Konkan Coast. We learn little of Kanhoji's life and battles from these books of history whether written by Indian or English historians. Malgonkar's *Kanhoji Angrey* is an exception. It is probably the only book that deals with Kanhoji's life, his background, his naval battles, and his complicated relations with the six other powers that contend for mastery of the west coast in the eighteenth century: the Mughals, the Siddies of Janjira, the Portuguese, the Dutch, the English, and the Marathas. In the pages of Malgonkar's book Kanhoji ceases to be a mere "pirate"; he becomes an admirable "maratha admiral." Malgonkar has done more than any historian to flesh out the character of Kanhoji, one of the most interesting historical figures of eighteenth-century India.

Little is known about the early years of Kanhoji Angrey, who was born in 1669. His father, Tukoji Sankpal, a roaming rootless soldier, sent him to a Brahmin teacher in Harnai Village to be educated. Malgonkar dismisses the legends about Kanhoji's childhood years as mere "cobwebs." When Shivaji died in 1680 Kanhoji was only 11 years old and was still at the house of the Brahmin teacher. Kanhoji grew up during a period of turmoil in India. The Marathas were at war with the Mughals, the Siddies, and the Portuguese; the Mughals were at war with the Bijapur kings, and the Dutch and the English traders were establishing firm footholds on the west coast. When Kanhoji was twenty-five he took part in naval engagements between the Siddy and Acholji Mohitay, the commander of Suvarnadurg, a fort about a hundred miles south of Bombay. After the engagement the monarch in appreciation of his courage gave formal command of the fort of Survarnadurg to Kanhoji.

Shivaji was succeeded by Sambhaji, who was captured, tortured, and put to death by the Mughals in 1687. Rajaram, his younger brother, became the regent and resumed the struggle with the Mughals in a war that was protracted interminably. He made many appointments of commanders: Siddoji Jujjar was granted the rank of *Surkhail* ("Grand Admiral") and was given the overall responsibility of defending the coast. Two Deputy Commanders were also named, one of them being Kanhoji Angrey. Later when Balaji Vishwanath became Peshwa under King Shahu, Kanhoji accepted Suzerainty of Shahu. In return Shahu entrusted Kanhoji with the task of guarding the coast as Surkhail. King Shahu and Kanhoji signed the Treaty of Colaba in 1714. Malgonkar says:

As a result of the Treaty of Colaba, Kanhoji obtained control of ten seaside forts and sixteen land forts; his annual income from the territory placed under his authority was thirty-six lakhs of rupees. He was confirmed as the *Surkhail* and *Vazarat Ma-aab* in hereditary perpetuity. From now on he signed all his correspondence as "Kanhoji, son of Tukoji, *Surkhail* by the grace of King Shahu," and his seal of office read: *Shahukarya dhurandar Tukoji tanujanmanah Kanhoji Surkhailasya Mudrikeyam Virajate.* (177)

Kanhoji was an astute diplomat. He recognized the overlordship of the Maratha kings and regents. Yet he flew his own bloodred standard wherever he lived. He possessed to a great extent many rare and undefinable qualities that make a leader. Malgonkar says:

A man of incredible stamina, bold, brave and independent; yet, a man of patience and cool judgment; a man who exuded a hairy-chested maleness, who laughed uproariously and danced and sang with his men, and who never hesitated to fling the same men into assaults against unknown odds; a man with the sternness and mental discipline to punish a spy or a traitor by ordering him to be trampled under an elephant's foot, and yet with the softness of heart to undertake to look after the man's wife and children. (170)

We know very little of his personal life. He had three wives and many concubines. He was the father of seven legitimate children and at least as many children from his mistresses. Fond of song, dance, and drama, he maintained a troupe of singers and dancers at his court. We do not know whether he liked alcohol in any form. He was fond of swords and horses, and paid fabulous prices for the swords of Toledo and Damascus and the best horses from Arabia. He also collected guns from England and would admire their finish and engravings as much as their performance.

To understand the place of this extraordinary man in Indian history it is extremely important to gain some sense of the prevailing conditions of India; more specifically of the west coast of India. At the beginning of the eighteenth century, Konkan, the rugged coastline about 400 miles long between Bassein and Karwar, became the scene of a contest among six powers (noted above) which led to the ultimate rise of the British Power in India. In the light of later events, we may justly regard this struggle as a picture of a struggle on a smaller scale of what was going on in the whole of India; it is a struggle that decided once and for all that the English were to become masters of India. Kanhoji Angrey clashed with all six contenders, and for a brief period in the early years of the eighteenth century there was little doubt about his being the supreme master of the coast.

If, however, in the first years of the eighteenth century, any of the foreign powers along the coast of Konkan had been asked to nominate a common enemy, none of them would have picked out either the Mughals or the Marathas. Their answers would have been the same: Kanhoji Angrey! . . . Whoever ruled the land, whoever lorded it over their trading settlements surrounded by ditches and walls, there were no two opinions as to who ruled the waters of Konkan Coast during the first years of the eighteenth century: Kanhoji Angrey. (7 - 8)

Who were the enemies that Kanhoji had to contend with for the control of the west coast? As we noted above, there were six powers that he had to take into account. Let us look at them briefly.

First, the Mughals. They maintained a vast army but no navy in the Deccan. The reigning Mughal emperor in faraway Agra was Aurangzeb (1618 - 1707), a Muslim fanatic in the predominently Hindu India who succeeded in making the Mughal collapse certain through his religious policies. The Marathas had a long and bitter war with the Mughals even after Aurangzeb's death.

Second, the Siddies of Janjira. Janjira, 30 miles south of Bombay, was an impregnable fortress, the home and headquarters of the Siddy Kassam Yakoot Khan. The rulers of Janjira came from Abyssinia as traders but in the days of Kanhoji had become firmly established as a small naval power on the west coast. Although the Siddies had many Marathas in their service, the sailors in their fleet mostly came from Africa. The Siddies and the Marathas were in a perpetual state of war with each other. Shivaji had invaded the Siddy's territory in 1648 and that was the beginning of the enmity between the Marathas and the Siddies. But the Siddies by themselves were never a threat to the Maratha power. Siddy Rasool Yakoot Khan made peace with Kanhoji and signed a treaty of peace in 1715.

Third, the Portuguese. The Portuguese were the first to find a new route to India — Vasco da Gama reached Calicut on the west coast on May 17, 1498. Gradually the Portuguese established a number of settlements in Goa, Diu, Daman, Bassein, Chaul, and Bombay. Though the earliest "intruders into the East" by the eighteenth century they were losing their influence and power. The Portuguese signed a treaty with the East India Company on August 20, 1721, to gain control of the Konkan Coast and divide it between the Portuguese and the English. But the treaty did not last long. The Portuguese regarded themselves as a cut above the English in India. The Anglo-Portuguese attack on Kanhoji in Colaba did not succeed. A treaty was signed between Kanhoji and the Portuguese Viceroy in 1722. Both Kanhoji and the Portuguese agreed to help one another against enemies.

Fourth, the Dutch. The Dutch, too, had come to India with commercial interests. They had an important factory at Surat but they were on the way out. They were concentrating on building an empire elsewhere. Kanhoji seized a Dutch warship of thirty guns in 1703 which angered the English, strangely enough, even though there was a perpetual feud between the Dutch and the English in India. In 1724 the Dutch attacked Gheria but Kanhoji's Subedar repelled the attack.

Fifth, the English. The story of the English traders is well known. It was in 1612 that the first English factory was established at Surat. In 1668 the East India Company acquired Bombay from Charles II, who had got it from the Portuguese as a part of the dowry of his wife Catherine of Braganza at an annual rental of ten pounds. Bombay later grew prosperous and superseded Surat as the chief settlement of the English on the west coast. This was the first piece of English territory on Indian maps: "the minute red patch on it would erupt and begin to spread and spread until the whole of India became the color that was to be known as 'Empire pink' " (90).

Kanhoji Angrey clashed with the East India Company many times. He seized a merchant ship at Calicut once which had six Englishmen on board. The company took a serious view of this and wrote a sharp letter to Kanhoji asking for the immediate release of the ship. Kanhoji sent back word that he would "give the English cause to remember his name" (102). A treaty was signed between Kanhoji and the East India Company under which the English made Bombay a neutral port and Kanhoji undertook not to molest foreign ships in sight of the harbor. In 1717 Kanhoji took the company's timber from its boats. When Governor Boone sent a letter of protest demanding the return of the timber as well as the seized ships, *Robert* and *Success,* Kanhoji replied: "As I had a great necessity for timber when the boat came from Surat, I brought her in, in a friendly manner, believing that you offered friendship" (193).

The East India Company attacked Gheria in 1718, also known as Vijay-durg. It was an attempt to destroy a large part of Kanhoji's fleet as it huddled up in its monsoon anchorage. Gheria, with no more than a hundred men, flung back a major assault by the English, inflicting more casualties upon them than the total number of fighting men in port. The second Gheria expedition by the English also failed. The Anglo-Portuguese attack on Colaba in 1721, as we have seen, did not succeed but resulted in a separate treaty between Kanhoji and the Portuguese, leaving the English out. The English sailed back to Bombay, their friendship with the Portuguese completely shattered by Kanhoji Angrey.

In 1724 Kanhoji wrote a letter to Governor William Phipps, offering his hand of friendship. In his reply Governor Phipps rejected the offer of peace. In 1728 Kanhoji captured the English ship *Derby* which was said to be the richest prize he ever took. This was the last ship he captured.

Sixth, the Marathas. As a Maratha himself Kanhoji recognized the Maratha King's suzerainty. Among the Indian powers the Marathas alone showed a great interest in the sea. Shivaji had built up a formidable fleet.

At the time of his coronation, Shivaji had 57 major ships of war . . . with a total fighting strength of over 5,000 men. Five years later, there were 66 major ships. Even his expedition to Karwar and Ankola nine years earlier had been mounted with 85 assorted *gallivats,* each ranging from 30 to 150 tons, and three masted *ghurabs,* with a total fighting strength of 4,000 men — a formidable force even by today's standards. (17)

As we noted earlier, Kanhoji signed the Treaty of Colaba in 1714 with King Shahu under which Kanhoji was appointed Surkhail.

The Marathas as people of this land of Konkan began to think that Konkan and its coastal waters belonged to them and to no one else. Kanhoji was perhaps one of the few who realized that the sea was free; that no one, whether English or Dutch or Portuguese, had a right to check his ships on the high seas.

This was the *dramatis personae* consisting of three Indian and three European groups of characters for a drama in which Kanhoji played an important role at the beginning of the eighteenth century. This drama produced lasting consequences for the whole of India; indeed, it was a turning point in Indian history. For a brief period Kanhoji was the master of the sea.

The British called him a land-shark who devoured everything on land as well as on water; they called him a robber, pirate, villain, rebel and sent emissaries to wait upon him with instructions to speak to him 'civilly' and make a fabulous offer to buy him off. The Portuguese called him even worse names and yet likened him to Barbarossa and sent him expensive presents (7)

Kanhoji's major achievement was that he built up a fleet of vessels and made it into a formidable naval force in Konkan. When he began he did not use his ships as a naval force but as a sort of coastal police, pouncing upon ships that did not carry Maratha papers. In the eighteenth century he represents the only Indian power that took interest in ships and the sea — the Mughals and the Siddies had little or no knowledge of naval tactics and battles. The only naval powers that he had to contend with were European — the Dutch, the Portuguese, and the English. Kanhoji as the commander of the only Indian navy was determined to enforce his authority along the coast. He offered all ships his permits, called *dastaks,* offering protection at sea from pirates. Ships without *dastaks* were seized. He knew that the *ghurabs,* the *gallivats,* the *pals,* and the *shibars* of his fleet were no match for the English or Portuguese ships which were handsome and better designed. The biggest *ghurab* was no more than 400 tons; frigates or *gallivats* were between 60 and 120 tons. He concentrated his energies on building bigger and better ships. He established five shipyards with hundreds of workmen and foreign experts to build new ships, and he even planted enormous tracts with teak.

Kanhoji's success against the superior ships and the superior arms of the English and the Portuguese can be ascribed to his special naval tactics. He kept his ships close to the coast because they could never achieve greater speed than European ships. His ships would swoop down upon European ships when they reduced sail and slowed down near the coast. His men were far superior in hand-to-hand fighting, in the use of the sword and the shield, to the European sailors.

Kanhoji groomed his eldest son Sekhoji to take his place after him. But his second son, Sambhaji, brave, ruthless, and ambitious, was not content to take a second place. Strife among his sons haunted Kanhoji in his later years. He was sad to see disunity in the house of the Maratha king himself — there were two Maratha kings and two kingdoms, one at Satara and the other at Kolhapur, both intriguing and fighting against each other. Kanhoji died with these haunting thoughts on July 4, 1729.

## II  *Puars of Dewas Senior*

Two Maratha brothers, Tukoji Puar and Jivaji Puar, founded the Maratha Kingdom of Dewas in Central India in 1731. Dewas in 1731 was a small village dominated by a massive hill, the hill of Devi. It is roughly in the center, barely twenty miles from both Ujjain and Indore. E. M. Forster in *The Hill of Devi* (1953) describes "the curious twin states of Dewas":

At the time I knew them, their territories were inextricably mixed with each other and with the territories of surrounding states . . . the two rulers made half-hearted attempts to escape each other's embraces. . . . A map of their possessions lies before me. The Senior Branch (tinted green) owned 446 square miles and had a population of 80,000, the Junior Branch (pink) was a little smaller. The district of Sarangpur (yellow) was administrered jointly — I know not how. . . . The area was divided between the two states not by towns or sections, but by fields and streets: In Dewas City, S. B. would own one side of a street and J. B. the other. The arrangement must have been unique and an authoritative English lady, who knew India inside out, once told me that it did not and could not exist, and left me with the feeling that I had never been there. . . .[2]

When the brothers found the dual rule impracticable they decided to divide their kingdom and establish a Senior and Junior Branch. They were descendants of Sabu Singh Puar who had helped Shivaji in 1657 in capturing Kalyan. Krishnaji, Sabubingh's son, too, was one of Shivaji's military commanders or sardars. When Rajaram was the Regent of the Marathas three Puar brothers — Bubaji, Rayaji, and Keroji — assisted him in resisting the enemy. During the reign of Shahu the Puars acquired power and prestige and were regarded as prominent Maratha families. Shahu's cause was upheld by the Puars. When Shahu and Balaji Vishwanath came to the momentous decision in 1714 to send out their forces into North India they selected Kaloji Puar as one of their commanders. The Marathas fought with the Mughals and brought more and more territories under their control. It had been the practice of the Marathas to allot newly won territories to the military commanders who won them. And so the Puars received the place called Dewas in 1731, where they established their headquarters.

The Puars continued to take part in the Maratha campaigns against Mughals, the Nizam, and the Portuguese. Tukoji Puar's column played an important role in the capture of Dharavi from the Portuguese in 1739. As a mark of appreciation of Tukoji's services in these battles King Shahu bestowed upon Tukoji Puar the hereditary title of *Senahaptasahasri* ("Commander of Seven Thousand").

Tukoji Puar's successor, his son Krishnaji I, took part in the great battle of Panipat in 1761 against Abmad Shah Abdally which resulted in the crushing defeat of the Marathas. It was the greatest pitched battle the Marathas had so far undertaken. It was a massacre of the Marathas, three out of every four died in the battle. Krishnaji I who was only 20 years old fought bitterly to the end. Out of his own 1000 troops only four horsemen had survived to return to the Dewas.

After Peshwa Balaji Rao's death his son Madhavrao, only sixteen years old, became Peshwa. Madhavrao's uncle Raghunathrao also wanted to become Peshwa. The feud between the Peshwa and his uncle became serious as years passed and developed into a civil war. Both parties made efforts to get the support of Krishnaji Puar and Jivaji Puar. Krishnaji and Jivaji remained steadfastly loyal to the Peshwa, who entrusted them with the task of "wiping out the stain of Panipat." The Marathas captured Delhi after a fight with the Mughals in 1771 and installed Emperor Shah Alam on the Delhi throne.

When Peshwa Madhavrao died without issue his uncle Raghunathrao saw his chance to become the Peshwa. He turned to English traders for help. They made a hard bargain with Raghunathrao offering him military help provided Raghunathrao paid all the expenses of the campaign and also ceded a territory near Salsette and Bassein. Colonel Keating signed a treaty with Raghunathrao on March 6, 1775. Krishnaji Puar was dragged into this war with the English which lasted seven years — the first Anglo-Maratha War (1775 - 1782). It was a crushing defeat for the English. They handed over Raghunathrao to the Marathas after the Wadgaon Treaty.

Krishnaji Puar helped Emperor Shah Alam in hunting down Ghulam Kadar who had made his bid to assume control of Delhi in 1787. The grateful Shah Alam singled out Krishnaji for rewards and honored him with "robes made of gold brocade" and presented him with a sword with his personal seal cut into it.

The Puars were also drawn into wars with the East India Company, which had not given up imperial ambitions after 1782. The company fought two wars which finally wiped out the kingdom of the Marathas: The Second Anglo-Maratha War (1803-1805) and the last Anglo-Maratha War (1817 - 1819). The Second Anglo-Maratha War was conducted in two main centers, in the Deccan under Arthur Wellessley and in the North under General Lake. Wellessley gained a complete victory over the combined troops of Marathas at Assaye. General Lake captured Delhi and Agra and the Marathas were severely routed. By 1818 the Marathas were no longer a power.

Over these years the process of land-grabbing went on with ever-gathering momentum and gradually the modest estates of the East India Company assumed the shape and substance of a new state. The Maratha Empire was broken up and the pieces of that Empire, together with Lucknow, Hyderabad, Mysore, became part of the empire of the East India Company. In 1818 the conquest was complete. (232)

The English were the new masters. A treaty between the East India Company and Tukoji Puar and Anandrao Puar was executed on December 12, 1818. Both the Puars were recognized as the joint rulers of Dewas and the entire Dewas state was administered through one Dewan. This arrangement was found unsatisfactory when Rukmangadrao Puar became the ruler.

The twin states came into being during 1840 - 45. Rukmangadrao's portion was called the *Bari-pati* ("Senior Branch"). Most of the territory of the state was divided but the two major towns, Dewas and Sarangpur, were ruled jointly still.

In 1861 Krishnaji Puar became the ruler of Dewas Senior. It was during his reign that even the towns of Dewas and Sarangpur were divided between the two families. The disputes between the families resulted in an extraordinary division. Dewas City was divided in 1886 and Sarangpur in 1889. As we have seen, E. M. Forster wrote about this division in *The Hill of Devi* (1953) as "unique."

Tukoji Rao Puar III succeeded to the throne at the age of eleven in 1899 and assumed full powers in 1908. Much is known about this prince because he was the subject of E. M. Forster's *The Hill of Devi* and Sir Malcolm Darling's *Apprentice to Power* (1966). E. M. Forster was Tukoji Rao's private secretary for six months in 1921, and Darling was his tutor. Darling's mother became his confidante. Complex, witty, a victim of harassment by the colonial bureaucracy, "certainly a genius and possibly a saint," Tukoji Rao became a good friend of both Darling and E. M. Forster.

Tukoji Rao became engaged to Akka Sahib, the only daughter of the Maharajah of Kolhapur. He paid frequent visits to Kolhapur before marrying the Kolhapur princess in 1908. The marriage was performed in the presence of a glittering collection of dignitaries, both British and Indian. As a present his father-in-law, the Chhatrapati of Kolhapur, a direct descendant of the great Shivaji, bestowed on Tukoji Puar the rare honor of carrying the *Morchals,* which, according to Maratha traditions, is the symbol of royalty itself.

Unfortunately the marriage did not succeed. Akka Sahib was not happy in Dewas. On April 4, 1910, a son was born to her in Kolhapur. When she went to Kolhapur on one of her visits in 1914, she decided to stay there permanently. No one knows exactly what went wrong. Perhaps the incessant quarrels of the old Dowager Rani or the domineering ladies of her husband's family forced her to make this decision. The separation left a deep gash on Tukoji's mind and turned the Kolhapur Chhatrapati against him.

Tukoji busied himself with the details of administration. In 1911 he was invited to attend the great Delhi Darbar held during the visit of King George V and was invested with the title of the Knight Commander of the Star of India. Later during the years of the First World War the government bestowed upon him the hereditary title of Maharaja in recognition of his services to the war effort. The British officials held him in high esteem. They liked his natural charm, quick intelligence, and his gaiety.

In 1926 Tukoji's son, Vikramsinharao, married Pramilaraje, the eldest daughter of the Raja Saheb of Jath. The wedding took place in the presence of a vast "concourse of nobles." The wedding was the last happy landmark of his life. His decline began after this event. He had spent a fortune on this wedding.

In 1927 Vikramsinharao left Dewas and began to live in Kolhapur with his mother. Then came the financial troubles. Tukoji was not a careful spender. His income from his lands, which had been ten lakhs, dropped down, and so he began to borrow money recklessly. In 1933 the Political Department of the government of India, taking a serious view of his indebtedness, called upon him to subject all his accounts to an accounts officer appointed by them. He did not answer but "took a final and fantastic step," as E. M. Forster wrote. He left Dewas to take refuge in Pondicherry, in French Indian territory.

The Political Department ordered him to return to Dewas. He merely sent a "thousand-word" telegram to the Viceroy, reiterating his determination to live in Pondicherry. The government decided to place the administration in the hands of his son, Vikramsinharao, who assumed his new office in 1934. On December 21, 1937 Maharaja Tukoji Rao died in Pondicherry.

Vikramsinharao Puar who later became the Maharaja of Kolhapur is today the true and only heir of Shivaji, the lord of all the Marathas. Born on April 4, 1910, and educated at Christian College at Indore, Vikramsinharao lived for a time with Sir Malcolm Darling as a member of their family and later with the family of noted educationist Professor P. E. Richards. He did remarkably well in sports, especially tennis. In Kolhapur his guardian was his maternal uncle, Rajaram Maharaj, who had succeeded Shahu Maharaj in 1922 as Chhatrapati.

After a period of administrative training under Dewan Sir Mirza Ismail in Bangalore, Vikramsinharao returned to Dewas on July 26, 1934, as the President of the Council of Members. As we have seen this was the time when Maharaja Tukoji Rao had left Dewas and was living in Pondicherry. When Maharaja Tukoji Rao Puar died on December 21, 1937, in Pondicherry Vikramsinharao Puar of Dewas Senior became the Maharaja. He held discussions with the Maharaja of Dewas Junior over exchange of fragmented territories. A formula accepted by both the branches of the family received British approval. The new divisions came into effect on September 14, 1940.

When the Second World War began Vikramsinharao sent a telegram to the Viceroy expressing his desire to serve personally in the war. On October 1, 1940, he joined the preparatory training course for officer cadets of Central India at Indore. On November 26, 1940, Chhatrapati Rajaram of Kolhapur died without an heir. Vikramsinharao became one of the candidates for the throne of Chhatrapati of Kolhapur being the nearest male relative of the late Rajaram Chhatrapati. The Senior Maharani, however, chose Nana Sahebe Bhonsle Chavrekar, renamed Shivaji, as the Chhatrapati on January 18, 1942.

Maharaja Vikramsinharao received his knighthood in June, 1941 and an Emergency King's Commission in August. He chose the Maratha light Infantry. He appointed his wife, Her Highness the Maharani Pramilaraje, to act as Regent during his absence. He sailed from Bombay on October 29, 1941, and arrived just in time in the Western Desert for one of the fiercest battles of "Operation Crusader," the Eighth Army's bid to drive Rommel out of Cyrenaica. On January 25, Maharaja Vikramsinharao was appointed the Brigade Liaison officer (BLO) and given the acting rank of captain.

Maharaja Vikramsinharao took over as President of Indore State Cabinet on September 20, 1942, when he returned from war on leave. He also took over the reins of administration of his own state of Dewas from his wife. In 1945 the Viceroy asked him to proceed to Italy and the Middle East to visit the Maratha units as well as all the units of the Indian State Forces and make a report on their morale and welfare. The Maharaja visited Florence, Naples, Rome, and Cairo and returned to India. He was promoted to the rank of Major in 1946.

On September 28, 1946 Chhatrapati Shivaji of Kolhapur died. This time Maharaja Vikramsinharao's claim to be considered as heir was recognized by Maharani Tarabai. He abdicated the Dewas *gadi* to become Chhatrapati of Kolhapur in 1947. He was renamed Shahaji Maharaj. His son Krishraji Rao III became the ruler of Dewas Senior on April 19, 1947. He was only fourteen years old.

Maharani Pramilaraje once again became the Regent. Great changes were taking place in India, which became independent on August 15, 1947. On June 27, 1948, Dewas Senior was merged in Madhya Bharat and in November, 1956, Madhya Bharat became part of Madhya Pradesh State of India. Kolhapur State also became integrated into Bombay State in 1949. Dewas Senior and Kolhapur were lost in the vast totality of India. The princely states have disappeared from the map of India, but the princes still hold a special place of respect in the hearts and minds of people of the states.

### III  *Chhatrapatis of Kolhapur*

The Maratha Kingdom of Kolhapur began as an independent kingdom in 1710, became a semi-independent princely state under the British in the nineteenth century, and merged into Bombay State in 1949. Between Shivaji I (1700 - 1714), its first Chhatrapati, and Chhatrapati Shahaji Maharaj (1947), its twelfth and present Maharaja of Kolhapur, lie two hundred and fifty years of history of twelve Chhatrapatis. This is the subject of Malgonkar's *The Chhatrapatis of Kolhapur* (1971). It is essentially the story of their rise and fall, their great achievements and faded dreams.

Kolhapur was established as a result of the dispute that arose over the claim for the kingdom of Chhatrapati Shivaji between the descendants of his two sons, Sambhaji and Rajaram. Sambhaji's descendants reigned over the Satara branch. As we have seen, Kolhapur's present Chhatrapati is the former ruler of Dewas Senior, Vikramsinharao Puar, who became the ruler of Kolhapur in 1947. The two ruling families came together earlier in 1908 when Tukojirao Puar III, Vikramsinharao's father, married Chhatrapati Shahu Maharaja's daughter, Akkasaheb, the Kolhapur princess.

Kolhapur, the capital of the Kolhapur kingdom for nearly two and a half centuries, forms the heartland of the South Western portion of the Deccan. When Shivaji, the founder of the Maratha empire, died in 1680 he left two sons, Sambhaji and Rajaram, but no decision as to his successor. A struggle for power began in Raigad, the capital. Sambhaji had himself proclaimed king. Aurangzeb, the Mughal emperor, had come to the Deccan with a vast army to crush the Marathas. He captured Sambhaji, inflicted barbarities on him, and killed him in 1687.

Rajaram, Sambhaji's stepbrother, was proclaimed regent. He was only seventeen years old. He made a dash to a fort called Jinji when Raigad was attacked by the Mughals. Aurangzeb ordered his Commander Zulfikar Khan to proceed to Jinji and to take the fort. Rajaram had himself proclaimed the Chhatrapati. Three men helped Rajaram to save the Maratha kingdom: Ramachandra Amatya, Santoji Ghorpade, and Dhanaji Jadhav. A secret understanding took place between Rajaram and Zulfikar Khan to share the land.

After Rajaram's death in 1700 his wife, Tarabai, a courageous and astute woman, played an important role in founding the Kolhapur dynasty. Tarabai fought the Mughals, defied many advisers, and refused to accept Sambhaji's son, Shahu, as the Maratha king and set up her own son, Shivaji I (1700 - 1714) as the real Chhatrapati. For fifteen years Tarabai dominated the Maratha history as Regent. From her headquarters at Panhala she sent orders even to Kanhoji Angrey. She received help from the Puar brothers, Kaloji and Sambhaji. She made Panhala, not Satara, the real capital of the Maratha kingdom, and her son was proclaimed as Shivaji I of the Kolhapur dynasty. Shahu's kingdom was ruled from another capital, Satara.

Sambhaji I (1714 - 1760) became the ruler after a coup which removed Shivaji I and Tarabai from power in 1714. Sambhaji carried on Shivaji's war against Shahu and his Peshwa, Balaji Vishwanath. On November 30, 1725, and April 13, 1731, there were two treaties between the warring cousins, Shahu of Satara and Sambhaji of Kolhapur, which put an end to their hostilities by a division of territories. The treaties recognized the two separate kingdoms and established the dividing line between them — the river Varna. North of this line was Shahu's kingdom, Satara; south of this line was Sambhaji's kingdom, Kolhapur.

Sambhaji I died in 1760. The great battle of Panipat in 1761 rocked the very foundations of Maratha power. Shivaji II, a young boy, was enthroned as Chhatrapati in 1762. Jijabai, Sambhaji's wife, preserved the Kolhapur kingdom from becoming extinct. After her death in 1773 Durgabai conducted the affairs of the state on behalf of the still youthful Shivaji who assumed full control of the affairs in 1779. In 1788 the capital of the kingdom was shifted from Panhala to Kolhapur. Shivaji II died in 1813, leaving thirteen wives, six daughters, and six sons.

Sambhaji II, the elder son of Shivaji II, became Chhatrapati in 1813. He was only a boy of thirteen. The period of disintegration of the Maratha confederacy and the takeover of the East India Company had begun. Kolhapur's effort was directed toward extracting the most advantageous terms from the British who had now become the unchallenged masters of the land. The British flag was hoisted even on the Peshwa's palace in Poona. Kolhapur ceased to be a kingdom. It was now a princely state, dependent on the British. Its borders were guaranteed by the overlords, the East India Company.

Shahaji I became Chhatrapati in 1821. He was faced with a good deal of opposition from the feudatories. His attack against Kagal in 1825 provoked British indignation, and the British pushed back the Kolhapur troops. A treaty signed by the British and Chhatrapati Shahaji reduced Kolhapur's troop strength. The British began to intervene in the internal affairs of Kolhapur, and they forced the Chhatrapati to accept their own nominee for a chief minster. A British garrison also came to Kolhapur.

Shivaji III (1838 - 1866), the next Chhatrapati, was only a boy of eight when he became Chhatrapati. For the thread ceremony performed in 1839 Kolhapur minted for the last time its own coins. The East India Company took complete control over the coinage after 1839. Some disgruntled soldiers made an assault on the chief administrator in 1844. The British acted with speed and vigor and rushed troops to Kolhapur from Belgaum and put down the revolt. All those who participated in the Kolhapur revolt were rounded up and imprisoned. The East India Company, which at this time before the mutiny of 1857 was mercilessly abolishing one state after another, was inclined to abolish or annex Kolhapur but did not do so. Kolhapur was allowed to continue as a princely state; however, the British decided to keep a British military force permanently in Kolhapur.

During the "Great Revolt of 1857" there was an uprising in Kolhapur in the form of an insurrection by men of the 27th Native Infantry. The Chhatrapati's brother Chimasaheb was one of the leaders of the revolt. The British officers in Kolhapur took refuge in Residency. On July 31, the 27th Infantry began to loot and go after their officers. By August 10, the British force was augmented by the arrival of a squadron under Lieutenant Kerr. The mutiny was quickly quelled by the British with additional reinforcements from Bombay. Colonel G. Le Grand Jacob kept up the climate of terror through acts of vengeance. Chimasaheb, the younger Maharaja, was secretly deported to Karachi. In 1863, when he was thirty years old, Shivaji III was invested with ruling powers; however, his chief administrator had to be acceptable to the British. Three years later on August 4, 1866, he died.

Rajaram I was adopted as the successor in 1866 when he was sixteen years old. Captain West introduced the Maharaja to the conduct of public administration. In May, 1870, Captain West and the Maharaja set out for a trip to Europe. Rajaram I died in Florence after a short illness on November 30, 1870. He had spent more than four months in England. The British political agent in Kolhapur, Colonel Andersen, managed the day-to-day administration. Shivaji IV became the Chhatrapati after an adoption ceremony in 1871 when he was only eight years old. The British continued to rule Kolhapur directly and to educate the boy Chhatrapati. Colonel West now became Shivaji's guardian. Shivaji was conferred Knight Commander of the Star of India at a special *durbar* on January 1, 1878. Later, the Prince is said to have shown signs of mental derangement. He was kept segregated from everyone. On December 25, 1883, Chhatrapati Shivaji IV died in Ahmadnagar as the result of injuries suffered at the hands of his keeper, Private Green. For two years Shivaji had been held captive in the Ahmadnagar fort.

Once again the question of finding a successor arose. Yeshwantrao was adopted and given the family name of Shahu Maharaj in 1884. *Chhatrapatis of Kolhapur* ends at this point even though the new Chhatrapati ushered in Kolhapur's most progressive and prosperous years. Kolhapur remained a princely state in the framework of British paramountcy for another sixty-five years and was integrated into Bombay State in 1949. As we have seen, Kolhapur like many princely states vanished into the vast totality of India.

An "Appendix" briefly surveys the reigns of the following: Shahu Chhatrapati (1884 - 1922), Rajaram II (1922 - 1940), Shivaji V (1942 - 1946) and Shahaji II (1947 - ). The book also includes two maps and a number of photographs of Chhatrapatis.

## IV    *Conclusion*

Malgonkar's three books of formal history rest on the research and scholarship of others, not his own. *The Puras of Dewas Senior* and *Chhatrapatis of Kolhapur* are in fact works of collaboration. Chhatrapati Shahaji Maharaj of Kolhapur himself is one of the collaborators. *The Puars of Dewas Senior* is primarily based on Mr. V. Gujar's *Sansthan Dewas Thorli Pati Puar Gharanyachya Itihas* in Marathi and the collection of papers published by him on the history of Puars. Gujar spent more than ten years in sifting the moldy records in various parts of India. Gujar's book on Chhatrapatis was also an important source for Malgonkar's *Chhatrapatis of Kolhapur*. Gujar sifted, collated, and edited a great mass of material and published it in eight volumes under the title (in Marathi) *Karveer Chhatrapati Gharanyachya Itihasachi Sadhane.* Mr. S. M. Garge's *Karveer Riyasat,* also in Marathi, is the principal source book for Malgonkar's *Chhatrapatis of Kolhapur.* Malgonkar depended also for his historical writings on what he calls "History Circle," a study and discussion group with Shahaji Maharaj as the presiding officer. Here at these long sessions every single fact was checked and cross-checked. Colonel Dinkar Kerkar did the maps for *Puars of Dewas Senior* as well as for *Chhatrapatis of Kolhapur.*

Malgonkar's reputation rests chiefly on his novels, not on his books of history. The books of history are important for what they reveal about his scholarly interests and intellectual preferences. They testify to his deep interest in Maratha history and to his gifts as a seasoned and accomplished storyteller. Critically, he cannot be ranked alongside the famous historians like Sarkar, Gibbon, or Churchill. Malgonkar's works of history often seem to be defending the princes. Nevertheless, his works have more than transient worth as they make the knowledge of Maratha history accessible to the English-speaking world for the first time.

These books invite us to meet Admiral Kanhoji Angrey, the rulers of Dewas Senior and of Kolhapur, and help us to understand their achievements and failures in the long history of India. Stylistically, too, these books are of interest for they show a novelist's way of dealing with formal history. Malgonkar finds in the Maratha history an interesting tale that needs to be told in English without, as far as possible, distorting historical facts. His history books, in this sense, read like novels. It should be added that Malgonkar has always regarded history and fiction as closely interrelated. He himself has moved from history (*Kanhoji Angrey,* 1959) to fiction (*Distant Drum,* 1960) and back again to history (*Chhatrapatis of Kolhapur,* 1971) and fiction (*The Devil's Wind,* 1972). He said in my interview with him:

"To my mind, history and fiction have not only many elements in common, history now forms the basis for most of my work. . . . I think the bonds of all fiction are these facts; and the facts are fantastic in Indian history, as they are in any history. . . . "

I asked, "Since you have done work both in professional history and historical fiction, do you think that history should be approached through both of these ways in order to get a balanced account of a

particular period? Should one turn to both formal history and
historical fiction?"

"I think historical fiction is a good way of making people swallow history.
Sometimes history seems too dry for the average reader, at least the way it is
written by most historians. I take pride in saying that when I write history I
make even history certainly readable. After all, there are characters in it;
they have feelings. Sometimes one is handicapped by the subject. Both my
books *The Puars of Dewas Senior* and *Chhatrapatis of Kolhapur* are commissioned works, they were not books I would have chosen to write. After
all, someone paid me a lot of money to write these books, and I was limited
by the characters and the nature of the subject.

At his best and at his worst Malgonkar's books of history, based
on the research of other scholars, and financially supported by the
ruling families about whom he was writing, and dedicated to the
present rulers of Dewas Senior and Kolhapur, appear to be works of
propaganda for the vanishing princes. The readers of scholarly works
of history miss in these pages the spirit of skepticism, perhaps the
most important historical tool for illuminating the past.

## CHAPTER 4

# The Princes (1963):
## *History in Fiction and Fiction in History*

*T*HE PRINCES (1963) is Malgonkar's most successful
novel. Its success at home and abroad, no doubt, is due
to his skill as a storyteller and to the fertility of his imagination. To
think of Malgonkar as solely, or even primarily, a purveyor of ex-
citing stories is, however, to do grave injustice to his true achievement. *The Princes,* viewed in a certain perspective, may be regarded
both as a document of contemporary history and as a work of conscious literary art. It is part fact, part fiction. For a great many of his
readers, the pleasure he principally offers is similar to that which the
treatment of historical subjects in fiction and on television provides
today. It is the pleasure from the insight and understanding he shows
in his interpretation of historical conflicts, from his ability to
penetrate to the human reality underlying those conflicts and the opposition of historical forces, and from the way he contrives to fuse, in
the creation of his fictional characters, their personal characteristics
with features and qualities that make them representative figures of
their times. One of the most interesting features of *The Princes* is the
fact that it is the portrayal of the recent past and of what Lukacs calls
the "present as history."

On one level the novel presents in fictional terms the central drama
of contemporary history — of recent Indian history of the decline
and fall of 565 princely states — in which the principal players were
the British, the princes, and the Congress Party. The characters are
modeled on real people and incidents closely resemble real events.
When the British left India in 1947, these 565 states were integrated
into the Indian Union within a matter of months. Molgonkar, the
novelist, was a witness to this brief but dramatic chapter of history,
and he treats just the thing that the student of history would like to
know — what kind of people were these ruling princes, how did they
treat each other, what did they think of the British and of the

Congress Party — often extending his observations to relationships inadequately documented elsewhere. On another level it is the story of His Highness, Maharaja of the clan of the Bedars, Hiroji the fourth, Knight Commander of the Star of India, of his palaces, tiger hunts, queens and concubines, and above all, of his son, Abhay, who goes through ceremonies of initiation and maturing and ceases to be a boy. Both themes — of Indian Independence and of the growing up of a prince — interweave and find their fullest expression in *The Princes*. Truth is skillfully interwoven with fiction; the growth of nationalism and the decline of the princely way of life are interwoven with the growth of a prince. In the interweaving of elements there is increasing complication but no petty mechanical balancing. The world of the old Maharaja was crumbling as the world of the young prince was being born. Here we have two opposed worlds or ways of life and characters who oscillate between them:

> He was the Maharaja with almost absolute power over five hundred thousand people; I was his heir. Imperceptibly the curtain thickened, and suddenly we were no longer merely a father and son, but a Maharaja and his successor. . . . I could not altogether push away the awful thought that he was someone who would have to die before I could come into my own. . . . Within ten years of my encounter with my father, the state of Begwad was merged with the vast totality of India. My father just missed being the last Maharaja of Begwad. I was the last, and it fell to me to sign that doleful document known as the instrument of merger, surrendering all powers as the ruler. (23-25)

*The Princes* can be summarized briefly. The scene is Begwad, a small princely state in the Deccan Plateau ruled by a Maharaja who upholds the *status quo*. ' "There will always be a Begwad, and there will always be a Bedar ruling it — so long as the sun and the moon go round!" ' (13). So he declared in the first scene to his son Abhay, the heir apparent, in 1938, when the tides of nationalist feeling, anti-British and antiroyal, were sweeping over India. This first scene in which the Maharaja and his son, Abhay, confront each other is, in a sense, the whole novel in miniature. We are introduced in this scene to a situation that is to be remedied, a conflict to be decided, and the themes to be developed. Abhay, not quite eighteen years old, sympathizes with the nationalists; his father who lived in a world of his own, remote from the twentieth century, has nothing but contempt for the nationalists who, under the leadership of Gandhi, were conducting campaigns for complete independence of India. Within ten years after this encounter the princely states were no more; they were merged with independent India. Abhay tells the story of these ten years in the first person:

The map was red and yellow. The red was for British India; the yellow for the India of the princes. . . . For more than a hundred years, the red and the yellow had remained exactly as they were. Then the British left, and in no time at all, the red had overrun the yellow and colored the entire map a uniform orange. The princely states were no more. We were the princes; no one mourned over our passing. . . . I realize that it could not have been otherwise, and yet I cannot rid myself of a purely selfish sense of loss. . . . (13)

## I.   The Princes *as Contemporary History*

Perhaps one way of understanding what Malgonkar has done in *The Princes,* as a preparation for assessing his achievement, is to concentrate in the first place on his raw material, that is, the historical facts on which the story of *The Princes* is based. The historical content supplies the spine of its narrative and the center of its interests. The novel evokes a comparatively recent period; he is writing of events that took place in India between 1938 and 1958, the years just before and after independence. When one considers *The Princes* in its entirety and Malgonkar's activities during these years as a professional big-game hunter proficiently tracking tigers for Indian princes, it is immediately apparent that he has drawn upon his own personal experience.

The historical record[1] is clear enough. Appendix 2, *India Before and After Independence,* see page 161, gives a brief summary of the events of the period. At the time of transfer of power from Britain to India and Pakistan in 1947 the only big question which remained to be resolved before August 15 was the future of 565 princely states occupying two-fifths of the land of the country and containing one hundred million people, just under a quarter of India's total population. On August 15 when British paramountcy was to lapse what would be the situation? Would the states become independent units even though they had never enjoyed this status? Would the British government hand over authority to their successors — India and Pakistan governments? Or would the princes decide whether they would continue as semi-independent states or join either of the two Dominions? Most of the states were situated within or adjoining Indian territory. The Indian government naturally expected that the princes would accede to the Indian Union. A small number of princes, with en-

couragment from political advisors, wanted to declare themselves independent, but a large number of princes were undecided.

The British government in their statement of February 20, 1947,
undertook not to hand over paramountcy to any government of
British India. In their view, on the lapse of paramountcy political
arrangements between states and the Crown would be brought to an
end. If nothing was done before August 15 to prepare for the situation the result would be political chaos. India would be Balkanized.
Lord Mountbatten, the Viceroy, persuasively urged on the rulers a
solution in the nature of a compromise between those who claimed
that the states would become independent and those who contended
that paramountcy must pass to the successor governments. He urged
the princes to sign a document called Instrument of Accession
thereby surrendering to one or another of the new dominions their
control over defense, external affairs, and communications.

On June 25, 1947, a "States Department" was created to deal with
all matters of common concern with the states, especially formula-
tion of agreements covering their immediate relations after the
transfer of power. Sardar Patel and V.P. Menon, who took over this
department, evolved a scheme for the integration of the states. The
department pressed for accession before August 15 with the direct
and personal assistance of Lord Mountbatten. On July 5, V.P.
Menon issued a statement in the name of Sardar Patel. It appealed
to the Rulers to accede to India only on three subjects — defense,
foreign affairs, and communications — and to come into the Indian
Union. It continued:

This country with its institutions is the proud heritage of the people who inhabit it. It is an accident that some live in the States and some in British India, but all alike partake of its culture and character. . . . It is therefore better
for us to make laws sitting together as friends than to make treaties as aliens.
. . . A great majority of Indian States have already come into the Constituent
Assembly. To those who have not done so, I appeal that they should join
now. The States have already accepted the basic principle that for Defence,
Foreign Affairs and Communications they should come into the Indian
Union. We ask no more of them than accession to these three subjects in
which the common interests of the country are involved. . . .[2]

Intensive, sometimes highly contentious, discussions followed this
statement of policy. July 25 was fixed for a conference with the
princes. On that fateful day Lord Mountbatten addressed the
Chamber of Princes as Crown Representative. Dressed in full uni-

form with an array of orders and decorations, the Viceroy spoke extempore and without any notes using "every weapon in his armoury of persuasion." V.P. Menon calls this speech the "apogee of persuasion."[3] Lord Mountbatten made it clear that the offer made by the Congress was most generous. He urged the princes to sign the Instrument of Accession before August 15. He would be unable to mediate between them and the Congress after August 15. This was their last chance. Lord Mountbatten continued:

. . . The states are theoretically free to link their future with whatever Dominion they may care. . . . May I point out that there are certain geographical compulsions which cannot be evaded. Out of something like 565 states, the vast majority are irretrievably linked geographically with the Dominion of India. . . . Remember that the day of the transfer of power is very close at hand and, if you are prepared to come, you must come before 15th August. I have no doubt that this is in the best interests of the States. . . . You cannot run away from the Dominion Government which is your neighbour any more than you can run away from the subjects for whose welfare you are responsible. . . .[4]

The Nawab of Bhopal who refused to attend this meeting felt, as he put it, that they were being "invited like the oysters to attend the tea party with the walrus and the carpenter." The Nawab had headed a group of rulers who opposed accession calling themselves "The Third Force." Leonard Mosley describes the meeting as follows:

Mountbatten . . . asked them to sign on the dotted line. He picked them out like school children and asked them whether they would sign. The expression on the face of even the richest of them was the sad, lost look of men in defeat. They had come to the meeting convinced that the Viceroy was going to save them and their privileges from the encroachment of the Congress vandals. . . .[5]

When the day for the transfer of power arrived — August 15, 1947 — barely three weeks after this masterly and momentous speech, every one except Junagadh, Kashmir, and Hyderabad had signed the Instruments of Accession. The Nawab of Bhopal's "Third Force" came to ruins. Later these three states too joined India. The political and constitutional chaos that might have followed the lapse of paramountcy had been averted. The Menon-Patel-Mountbatten team succeeded in integrating 565 Indian States in less than three weeks. August 15, 1947, marked the end of the British Raj and the beginning of free India and Pakistan.

What was true of most of the princes and their states is also true of His Highness The Maharaja of the clan of the Bedars, Hiroji the Fourth, Knight Commander of the Star of India, and his son, the narrator of *The Princes,* His Highness The Maharaja of Begwad, Abhayraj Bedar III. No matter how much Malgonkar may have altered or condensed specific details, *The Princes* is without doubt the fictional treatment of the plight of the princes who disappeared from history. E.M. Forster noticed some similarities between his own experiences in an Indian State recorded in *The Hill of Devi* and *The Princes.* In a letter he wrote to Malgonkar he says:

"I have just finished *The Princes* and should like to thank you for it. It interested me both in its own account and because I am involved — as far as Englishmen can be — in its subject matter. I happen to have been in touch with a small Maratha state (Dewas Senior) during the years of its dissolution. The parellels are numerous and heartrending. I am so glad you have got down a record. Otherwise all would soon be forgotten."[6]

Malgonkar told me that he wrote to Forster that he (Forster) had stayed in the same Indian state that he (Malgonkar) had written about. When I said that E.M. Forster's prince in *The Hill of Devi* reminded me of Hiroji, The Maharaja of Begwad in *The Princes,* Malgonkar said:

"It is surprising that you should mention it, because I also know the very same prince of the very same state very well. The prince that E.M. Forster knew died soon after Forster's visit. And his son, who became Maharaja after him, is a great friend of mine, and I am friendly with him today. So I couldn't take liberty with the characters and lie about my friend's father. But I am familiar with the state and whatever comparisons you see are perhaps real; I may have drawn something from my experience, which is also E.M. Forster's experience."

Speaking of the process of turning a real person into a fictional one in *The Princes,* of the relationship between the historical prototypes and the characters Malgonkar said:

"Well, I thought they were sufficiently camouflaged for you not to think of them as real persons. They are actually composite personalities, you know, there is no real person. I might disguise the voice or size of the person and put them into a character which has absolutely no connection with that person.
    Now many people think that the people in *The Princes* are real people. Now I think most novelists will never admit that they have used real people

in their novels. And I don't think it is true because in reality people are rather colorless. And if one of their aspects is especially worthy of putting into a novel certainly as a character you can not put a real person into a book, or hardly ever. You have got to sort of make composite characters — take the physical features from one, the peculiarities of another, character from someone else. But at the same time even as they emerge as types, they look like very live characters and people start identifying themselves with [them]: "Oh, this must be this man, I know him very well because of the way he talks and he has bad manners." So they keep asking me, "Is this true that you have written about any particular person?" But at the same time I have taken a lot of incidents and put them together and produced my characters. But when people start mixing your characters with real people it is a very flattering thing for an author.

Now John Marquand, an American author whom I have always admired, has somewhere said that the creative author is the closest thing to God on this earth. How is he the nearest thing to God? He creates characters which to many are actually real people because after all many readers think that the characters in a book are real people and they feel elated when the characters do very well, when they pass an examination or fall in love with the right girl. . . .[7]

Malgonkar's association very early in his life with the princes is clear from his statements and from two of his books of "straight" history dealing with the life and times of the princes — *Puars of Dewas Senior* and *Chhatrapatis of Kolhapur*. He said in our interview:

"My grandfather was the prime minister in one of the bigger states in India and I grew up . . . knowing the princely ways, knowing their peculiarities, knowing the little things that they did different from other people, knowing their little vanities. But that contact grew when I started my profession as a big-game hunter . . . anyway, I was for a little while a professional big-game hunter and my clients were the most monied one could think of, were American millionaires or Indian princes and one of them invited me to write the history of his family. So that gave me long enough contact, close contact with his family and with their attitudes and with their peculiarities to be able to write a book about princes."

*The Puars of Dewas State Senior* and *Chhatrapatis of Kolhapur* shed a good deal of light on Malgonkar's treatment of his raw material in *The Princes*. And so does E.M. Forster's *The Hill of Devi*. What Malgonkar has done is to take the authenticated facts of the State of Dewas Senior, its Maharaja, and his son, and camouflage them through the transforming power of novelistic imagination. In his hands facts become fiction. Perhaps this reshaping of fact into fiction can be clarified by pointing to some examples. Malgonkar transformed His Highness Sir Tukoji Rao III, K.C.S.I., Maharaja of Dewas State Senior into His Highness Sir Hiroji, the Fourth, K.C.S.I., Maharaja of Begwad, and his son Maharaja Vikramsinha Rao, later called Chhatrapati Shahaji, into Abhayraj Bedar III. There are no doubt discrepancies in detail between the facts and the fiction but in essentials history looks remarkably like fiction. Both Tukoji and Hiroji had feuds with Brahmin priests regarding their caste status, financial troubles because of reckless spending, and difficulties with their wives.[8] Chhatrapati Shahaji Maharaj and Abhayraj, on the other hand, have some similarities also — both were educated by English tutors, both went to college, both made concessions to the rising tide of democracy in their states, and both became officers in the British Army during the Second World War.[9]

Nevertheless, Hiroji and Abhayraj are not historical persons but creatures of imagination. In *The Princes* Malgonkar recreates an historical situation, places fictional characters in it, and describes how they behaved. But in *The Devil's Wind* he reverses the order; he takes a famous historical person, Nana Saheb, plunges him into fictional adventures, and puts into his mouth words for which there is no documented evidence. It is important to stress this distinction especially in considering the two major characters of *The Princes* — Hiroji and Abhayraj. They are essentially fictional portraits no matter how many similarities between them and their historical prototypes one might detect. But their historical situation is a different matter. The novel brings to life in very human dimensions the turbulent period before and after independence. Malgonkar does not tamper with the situation. The documented facts, the dates, the conferences between the princes and the Viceroy, the Privy Purses and so forth, as can be seen in the Appendix 2, *India Before and After Independence at a glance,* are carefully handled, without compromising history for the sake of the story at hand. The atmosphere of India is realized in a masterly fashion. When dealing with the historical situation of 565 princes Malgonkar does not make departures from the factuality of history. The princely states were ceded to India in return for a few perquisites and privy purses. The rulers first signed the Instruments of Accession and then signed the Instruments of Merger, which resulted in the merger of small states into a larger federation of states. All were finally swallowed into the belly of India. Malgonkar takes no liberties with these and other facts connected with the princely states. One glance at the Appendix 2 will establish this point. Lord Mountbatten addresses the Chamber of the Princes on July 25, 1947, for instance, both in history and in *The Princes.*

## II   The Princes *as Initiation Story*

To talk about *The Princes* in terms only of contemporary history, however, is to talk about one half of the novel. Contemporary history is no more or less important than the story of Abhayraj, the narrator. Unlike many contemporary novels based on topical events, *The Princes* is not just a recreation of a time, a society, and its social arrangements that are now history. *The Princes* is also the initiation story of Abhay, his growth from boy to man. Malgonkar has skillfully interwoven the historical theme into the initiation theme. The two plots — the public and the personal — run parallel to each other.

Much recent criticism of fiction has used the term "initiation" to illuminate hitherto unnoticed or misunderstood aspects of a literary work. We attain a new perspective if we think of Mark Twain's *Huckleberry Finn,* Stephen Crane's *The Red Badge of Courage,* or Hemingway's "The Killers" or Anderson's "I want to know why" as initiation stories. Manohar Malgonkar's *The Princes* seems to fall most naturally into place with these initiation stories. Abhay, the young hero, like his companions of these initiation stories, Huck, Henry Fleming, Nick, and the boy, has an encounter with the adult world, undergoes experiences that reveal hitherto unrecognized and uncomprehended aspects of the human condition, and emerges from the experiences chastened and wiser in the ways of the world. He completes his long, arduous, and at times disillusioning initiation before our eyes in *The Princes.*

*The Princes* is the story of a young prince's education. The kind of education Abhay undergoes is that known throughout the ancient world and primitive societies as "initiation." Malgonkar's construction of the story follows in detail the traditional formula of the myth. The progressive movement of the hero, as in all myths, is that of separation, initiation, and return. Within this general framework, Malgonkar plots his story with individual variation. Abhay, the youth, ventures forth from his known environment encountering the forces of sex, war, and death; he is transformed through a series of rites and revelations into a hero and returns — more as his father's peer and successor than as his son — to identify his new self with the deeper communal forces of the adult group.

Modern critics of the myth use the term "initiation" in many senses and for many purposes. The prevalence of imprecise criticism employing the concept of initiation suggests that the term requires clarification. For the sake of convenience and clarity, I propose to examine Abhay's initiation as a process consisting of six stages of growth and development. First, Abhay at eleven is initiated in a ceremony by his father. Second, he is instructed by his peers and teachers at school. Third, he emancipates himself from his tyrannical father in open revolt against him. Fourth, he is initiated into premarital sexual knowledge by Minnie Bradley. Fifth, he learns from his travels and actions in the war. And finally, he returns to the adult group and acts like his deceased father, identifying himself more and more with his views and values. Thus Abhay's changes in his social status from boyhood to adulthood are marked by a number of events rather than by any single dramatic ceremonial observance. Abhay is not regarded as a child one day and as a man the next. Such a conclusive recognition of adulthood is only possible in a less complex society. Certainly in our modern society the assumption of adult status is never a single definitive act. The initiation of Abhay is a prolonged and complicated process; it is not achieved by opening a door but by traversing a corridor.

Though Abhay's initiation is a process rather than an event, it begins with an initiation ceremony, which, like the initiation rites of most primitive cultures, centers around his passage from adolescence to maturity and full membership in adult society. The process involves isolation, ritualistic use of food, physical torture, and indoctrination in secret knowledge. Like the initiation ceremonies of an earlier society, Abhay's, directed by his father, begins with his removal to a secluded and sacred place, far from his mother and childhood associations. It is here that he receives the knowledge with which he can become a man. Abhay was eleven years old when he wept for his pet ram, Cannonball, which was wounded and killed in a fight with another ram, Sandogama. Tears flowed down Abhay's cheeks when he saw his brave Cannonball lying on the grass, his legs jerking and the blood spurting from his jet-black mouth and ears. That very evening his father, the Maharaja, took him to a dark room, asked him to sit in a high-backed chair, and said, holding a glass of whisky before him:

"It is a man's drink. . . . Men who weep cannot call themselves men. . . . We are like lions, we do not weep for dead lambs. . . . We never break down in public. There are in everyone's life, moments when it is much easier to weep;

but it is always more manly not to. Sorrow, grief, is a private thing, like . . .
making love.
"Yes, Dada" . . .
"It is most important not to squeal, to show hurt. Be a man, my son. . . . Will
you promise that you will never break down; at least when you are not by
yourself."
"Yes, Father". . . .
"Now drink this," Father said, and held the glass before me. "Drink it all
down, and then we will go down to the banquet. . . . " (32 - 33)

At the banquet the main dish of the evening was the cooked Cannonball. The Maharaja carved out the eyes from the head of the sheep
and handed them to Abhay to eat. Abhay grabbed the eyes firmly
with his fingers and thrust them into his mouth and then drank
another glass of whisky: " 'Make me a Man, O Lord,' I said to
myself. 'Make me a Man.' Was this what it involved, the process of
becoming a man? . . . " (35). Abhay's initiation ceremony shows
adult society testing his endurance and indoctrinating him. But it
does not carry him firmly into maturity and understanding; it only
leads him up to the threshold, leaving him enmeshed in a struggle for
certainty and self-discovery. Abhay takes his first tentative step
toward maturity under the tutelage of his father. But he still has to go
through a variety of experiences, pleasant and unpleasant, to complete his initiation into this select group. At the age of eleven Abhay
is decisively embarked toward the adult world, but still distraught
and struggling to adjust to his new knowledge (like the boy at the end
of "I want to know why"). Though Abhay eats the eyes and drinks
the whisky, his hatred for his father grows:

I kept my promise. I did not break down, and I felt a surge of triumph. I had
met the challenge thrown at me by a hated adversary.The victory was mine.
But that was one time I could have cheerfully killed my father; I, who loved
him and revered him all my life. (35)

One of the chapters of *The Princes* entitled "The Education of a
Prince" — a title that might well serve as the title of the novel —
deals with Abhay's growing-up years at school where we see him
breaking away from the ways of a child and learning the ways of an
adult. During this second phase it is his peers and teachers, not his
father, who are the major instructors, and especially Kanakchand,
his schoolmate; Mr. Frederick Moreton, his English tutor; Mr.
Walter Ludlow, the headmaster; and Hamidulla, his riding teacher.
Kankchand, the poor untouchable cobbler's son, was Abhay's "first

direct contact with the quivering poverty of India" (49). Abhay gave Kanakchand his own books when he realized that Kanakchand was too poor to buy them for himself. Mr. Moreton appreciated Abhay's generous act:

"It is one of the most satisfying things in life to be able to give someone what he really needs; only it takes a long, long time for most of us to find out. . . . I am really pleased you thought of giving your own books to the boy." (47)

Abhay admired Mr. Moreton very much and even later when he had grown up:

I now feel he may have been the greatest single influence of my early days. He was perhaps the only man in the palace who treated me as an equal, not as a child, but as an adult and, for much of the time, not as a prince either, but an ordinary man. He was always interested in what I had to say. . . . Even though he represented authority, I found myself regarding him more and more as a guide and mentor, even as a companion. (40 - 41)

When Abhay first heard the word "bastard" used by Kanakchand for Charudutt, Abhay's half-brother, it was to Moreton that he turned for explanation because he did not understand the word. Mr. Moreton after explaining said, " 'It is not a word that people . . . Well, people like ourselves, use . . . not a nice word' " (43). Mr. Walter Ludlow, another great influence, taught Abhay a few rules which helped his process of inculcation of socially approved virtues:

He had simplified life for all of us, reducing both religion and ethics to a few simple maxims. . . . "We have all come here with dealt-out hands," the Head would say. "And some of us may be holding better cards than the others. I don't care as much about whether you play your cards well or badly as about whether you play them honourably. That is what you are going to be taught here." And the one thing he was intolerant of was snobbery. If any of his students had any differences, they were made to settle them with their fists, in the boxing ring, and afterwards made to shake hands and forget all about the differences. (78 - 79)

Abhay's growing-up process at school, like that of most boys in modern society, involves spur-winning. He measures himself against the strength of his peers, of his older half-brother, even of his father. In American society a boy wins his spurs by selling newspapers, mowing lawns, shoveling snow off sidewalks, or doing some odd summer jobs. Abhay's spur-winning experiences, on the other hand, were involved with studies and sports; he managed to hold his own in his studies, and to captain both the cricket and hockey elevens. When the holidays came he wanted to "blood" his Holland, a shotgun his father had given him as a present. It was his favorite gift, and he had fondled as if it were a living thing. But he was shocked and enraged to discover that Abdulla Jan, the Palace Officer of whom his mother was fond, had used it:

I was like a strange man even to myself, cold, deliberate even in the grip of seething anger. Without a word, I picked up the Holland and broke it and inserted two number four cartridges and snapped the barrels home while he stood stock-still. . . .
I held the barrels pointed at his stomach, and he must have heard the snap of the safetycatch going forward. I was fifteen years old, nearly as tall as he was, and I was conscious that I was doing what I was doing not for my own sake but for the honour of our state. (83)

The Prince's education also consisted of riding, boxing, and music lessons, even lessons in wielding a sword. His father and his teachers had laid down a rigid timetable for his upbringing. An incident took place soon after the gun incident which shows Abhay as a skilled rider. He pushed aside Hamidulla, his riding instructor, adjusted the stirrups himself, and rode away bent forward like a professional jockey in a flat race, crashing through the stubble and thorn, accepting the challenge of the fences. He even rode over the black nullah, a death trap, where his Uncle Asokraj was killed some years before. Hamidulla, who had taught him all he knew about riding and horses, said with a look of approval, "You have certainly learnt all that I can teach you about riding and horses. There is nothing more I can teach you" (88).

The third phase of his initiation is an open revolt against his tyrannical father, an assertion of his manhood. It happened when Abhay was in his last year at college, not quite eighteen years old, and after he had won his spurs. One can view this rebellion as part of his quest for identity, of that ceaseless probing and parrying by which a young man comes to discover who he is. The Maharaja and his son clash in a scene set in the very beginning of the novel. They were talking about the rise of the nationalists. This first scene, in a sense, is the whole novel in miniature; it forecasts the novel's two themes: the growth of India's nationalism and the growth of a prince. The

Maharaja, who is old, reactionary, and taboo-ridden, has nothing but contempt for the nationalists. Abhay, on the other hand — young, progressive, and rational — has deep sympathies for them. Abhay goes on contradicting his father, questioning his privileges as the ruler, his faith in the British, and his confidence that the princes were meant to go on for all time, until his father loses his temper and says, "Is nothing sacred to you? . . . I think you have said quite enough, . . . Get out of my sight — at once!" (19). The time had come for his father to note that his son had come of age. From that moment they were no longer merely father and son, but a Maharaja and his successor. The Maharaja recognizes the process of awakening identity in his son, "It is surprising how quickly the horns grow on the foreheads of lambs" (17). This scene marks the end of one stage and the beginning of another in the process of Abhay's growing up. He was no longer tied to his mother's apron strings, nor a father-worshipping, uncertain, and naive youth at the threshold of maturity:

That unhappy scene in the room with the fifty-eight dead tigers and the old swords and shields nailed to the walls was like the ending of a phase. For many years from that day, our relationship became even more coldly formal than before. Whatever had held us close had broken away, only the shell of our proprieties now kept us together, like two men living under a flag of truce. (24)

During the fourth phase, Abhay is initiated in premarital sexual desire and knowledge by Miss Minnie Bradley, an English girl whom he met when he visited Simla for an interview. The princes, relaxed and permissive, did not crack down on sexual expression before marriage; they had a custom of providing young men with healthy concubines. When Abhay was presented with Zarina, a young concubine, he sent her away because he was deeply in love with Minnie, his "first successful encounter in the war of sex" (148). He had met her in a bar in Simla, and he could not take his eyes away from her; she was "somehow a part of the morning, of the verve and vitality of spring, volatile and blooming . . . slim as a bamboo and fresh as the morning dew" (131). He was hit by her earthly sensuousness: "At the same time I did not think that she was either beautiful or appealing. My only feeling was one of anger and annoyance, and yet she must have left a wealth of desire somewhere within me" (132).

He was very nervous when he took her out a few days later. It was a marvelous feeling, taking out a girl for the first time. He was only nineteen, but she was twenty-one. They enjoyed dinner, music, and dancing. Abhay enjoyed holding Minnie's warm hand in his own. He enjoyed her perfume and the brushing of her hair against his cheek. Before the evening was over he gathered her in his arms and kissed her: "That day was ours, Minnie's and mine, and for me it was a day of growing up, of coming of age, almost discovering myself . . ." (145). "I held her head in my hands and kissed her hard on the mouth. I had never imagined that a kiss would be such a searching, revealing, intimate experience. . . " (146).

He longed for Minnie when he went back to his palace in Begwad; he wrote letters to her and carried her picture with him even to the wars. His longing for Minnie formed the background to all his thoughts; he desired her and loved her with a passion he had never known. Months later he proposed to her and was determined to marry her. But the Maharaja intervened:

"For people in our position," my father began, "marriage is a sacred thing. It is not a private, purely personal matter at all, but an affair of state, as it were. Even the Political Department has an interest. There is a duty, an obligation, to marry someone suitable. Someone whom the people will one day have to accept as their Maharani." (168)

The Maharaja wanted Abhay to choose a girl from the royal families. He even sent his Chief Minister, Lala Harikishore, to meet Miss Minnie Bradley and offer her ten thousand rupees for Abhay's compromising letters. The Maharaja also had an alternative suggestion — she could go on living with Abhay as his mistress, in a "sort of unsanctified marriage." But Abhay was determined to marry Minnie. It was only later, during the war, that he made the shocking discovery in a letter that Minnie had written to Tony Sykes, her English friend, that his love — that is, Abhay's love — meant "nothing" to her. Tony, whom Abhay had seen die on the battlefield, brought him not only this disillusioning experience, but also a sense of humility:

Oddly enough, it was of Tony that I kept thinking, not Minnie. He had never once given me an indication that he was in love with her. . . . Nor had he even shown any illwill towards me. Ours had grown into a clean, purely professional relationship, untainted by rivalry . . . he was a man complete in himself; he was the prince, not I. And if he was in love with Minnie and she was with him, it was I who was the outsider, the third man. I felt no bitterness. I sat for a time, overcome by the aura of humility which death leaves in its wake. . . . (211)

In the fifth phase, Abhay is initiated by his travels. Soon after his return from Simla, he was made a cadet sergeant half-way through the course. His first post was at the Satpura Regimental Center at Raniwada. Here he kept a large mounted photograph of Minnie in a silver frame in his room; he often gazed at her and compared her to the two girls his father had chosen. Their photographs he had torn to pieces. After six weeks in the Regimental Center he was posted at a battalion in the Fourteenth Division in the Chindwara jungles very close to the war, where he was "stripped for action," forced to live under canvas, and to move from place to place. For days on end he had to subsist on hard rations and one bottle of water a day, which included, too, what he used for shaving. He continued to keep Minnie's photograph with him, the only link with the civilized world:

My impressions of the days in the training camp were overshadowed by an awareness of a total breaking away from my roots. It was almost as though I were a fugitive, leading a new life under a new name, a second lieutenant Bedar of the Satpura Rifles. My father had not written to me since I left home. . . . I willingly, almost eagerly, surrendered to the daily fatigue of mind and body, thankful for . . . the quick, unnoticed turning of day into night. . . . (179)

Late in the year 1941 Abhay was sent to the Intelligence School at Karachi. His father had used some influence to get him this post. He did well and managed to get a "D" or "distinguished" grade. He then asked to be sent to an active regiment, and he reported for duty to the Ninth Battalion of the Satpura Regiment at Mungad in the heart of the Deccan. After weeks of training the battalion was sent to Burma. Abhay, who usually measured up to the vicissitudes of war and life, was gradually transformed by his experiences:

The next few weeks are a blur on my memory, a patchwork of events and impressions and purely reflex action, of hurry and swearing, remorse and anger, hunger and fear, frustration and the quick dehumanization of war. We occupied new positions, only to abandon them a few hours later. . . . We tried to rally the spirits of our men, broken not so much by their rude baptism of fire as by the shock of being witness to the shattering blows inflicted on something that they had been taught to regard as inviolable. . . . Throughout our eight months in Burma, we were hardly ever out of contact with the enemy for more than three nights at a time. . . .

I remember living wholly in the present, more distressed about having to go without today's breakfast than about tomorrow's river-crossing. . . .

And yet sometimes . . . I would feel a lump rising in my throat, for death was one thing when you saw it in the streets, but quite another when you came across it in your shelter, in your own trench. I discovered for myself what many fighting men have written about, that you can take love to war, nursing it, magnifying it, even making of it a shield round you and believing yourself immune to the bullets because of it, but you cannot take hatred. . . .

I discovered that I no longer had any hard feelings towards my father, nor did I dislike Tony Sykes as much as I had expected. Now that I think of them together, they seemed to share a number of traits: disdain for danger, a capacity for coolness under stress, an unfailing readiness to take responsibility, and above all, a stubborn, almost stupid refusal to bend under pressure. (198 - 200)

Abhay won a Military Cross for his bravery in the war and was sent back to Karachi in 1942. It is here that he read in the Sindh Observer that Minnie had married Captain Farren, an aide-de-camp to the Governor of Bombay. His father was very proud of him when he returned home. It was almost two years since he had been home. " ' Back from the wars our conquering hero,' " said his father putting his hand on his shoulders. Like Stephen Crane in *The Red Badge of Courage* (1895) or Ernest Hemingway in *A Farewell to Arms* (1929), Malgonkar portrays his young protagonist returning home, shedding illusions about himself and about war, experiencing a new knowledge about the world. Abhay's eyes are gradually opened to the injustice and corruption beneath the glittering surface, and he emerges from the experience of war and travel, chastened, maturer, and wiser in the ways of the world. When Lala Harikishore handed him the packet of his letters to Minnie which had cost fifteen thousand rupees, Abhay thanked him:

She always had an instinct for business, Minnie, and I could not help admiring the way she had handled this; a complication of life neatly turned into a profit. For fifteen thousand rupees she might just get a small house in some cantonment town. Minnie always had a cool head, so inconsistent with her hesitant, helpless air. She had come out very well, all things considered. . . . Fifteen thousand rupees was cheap; yes, definitely so. (219)

Abhay at the end of the fifth phase put away childish things and moved from innocence to knowledge. He became a man.

In the sixth and final phase, the return of the initiates involves, in the language of myth, an identification with the adult males of the society and their values. And this is precisely what Abhay, the new Mr. Abhayraj, does — he marries Kamala, one of the two girls whose photographs he had thrown into his waste paper basket, and horsewhips Kanakchand, now a minister in the new cabinet, the same Kanakchand his father had horsewhipped years before. He became the spit and image of his father:

> Indeed it seems to me that with the passing of years, I have come to identify myself more and more with those values, with the result that today I feel myself a spokesman for whatever the princely order stood for.
> "Maharaja Abhayraj proved to be just as much reactionary as his father," the Settlements Minister wrote in his memoirs. He was referring to me, of course, and instead of feeling resentful, I was elated by the rebuke, proud of being thought like my father.
> Towards the end I was to become just as proud of our heritage as my father had been, the only difference being that I was prepared to take everything just as it was. . . . (20 - 21)

Abhay's marriage to Kamala took place in 1943. He gave consent by letter without even asking to see another photograph or to see the girl. It was a conventional Hindu marriage, like that of his father to his mother, a family alliance brought about by the pundits matching horoscopes. But the marriage turned out to be a happy one:

> When I reflect on this, I wonder whether there might not, after all, be something to be said for our deeply rooted customs, evolved after generations of trial and error; mine is certainly not an unusual example of how love can flow as a consequence of marriage, living together and the begetting of children.
> I first saw Kamala during the actual wedding ceremony. . . . I was conscious of my own emotional detachment, knowing that I was going through the ceremony as a sort of penance. It merely emphasized that I was now back within the fold, aware of my obligations to my inheritance. . . . (220 - 221)

Mr. Abhayraj had grown to resemble his father. As the main action of the novel progresses one is struck, not with the difference between them, but with the similarities. As the son grows he takes on more and more of the traits of his father. Late in the novel Abhay acts exactly like his father in a second horsewhipping incident. In the first of the incidents, placed at the beginning of the novel, the Maharaja, his father, had whipped Kanakchand, a poor untouchable student, for cheating and for wearing the white cap of the nationalists at the Asokraj High School. More than ten years later Abhayraj whips Kanakchand, now a minister in the new administration, at the same school, now called The National High School. Abhay now is exactly the same in pride as his father had been nearly ten years before:

> The scene was something I had seen before, many years earlier . . . there were streamers of buntings . . . arches made of bamboos and hoardings of welcome . . . there was even the faint trace of khas in the air — everything was the same. . . . I felt a black rage sweep over me, hitting me almost with a physical force. . . . I vaguely remember pushing through the throng . . . clutching the riding crop in my hand. I saw him close . . . cowering, shrinking, frightened; the face of a schoolboy in the grip of terror. I raised the crop high. I brought it down. (342 - 45)

Abhay is an extension of his father, and Kamala, Abhay's wife, notices this. She says, " 'sometimes you act so much like your father that it makes me feel frightened . . .' " (318). Malgonkar employs the device of repeated incidents, like the horsewhipping incidents, to emphasize the likeness between the Maharaja and Abhayraj. There are many more such repeated incidents in *The Princes*. For example, their visits to the fort of Patalpat where the Jamdar-Khana, the family treasure, was hidden. The treasure of the Bedars had been put together as the result of five generations of plunder. There were jewels, ornaments, precious stones, and swords estimated to be worth between five and six crores of rupees. Yet they carry away one article at each visit. When Abhay visited this secret place protected by the Ramoshis, the men who had guarded the treasure for two hundred years, he picked up a wheel-lock pistol from its velvet case and brought it out. Later in the novel Abhay learns that the pistol was one of a pair. His father had brought out its twin when he had visited the Jamdar-Khana:

> Father said, ". . . I brought out its twin when I went in as a young man. I did not feel like taking anything else. Now you have got the other. . . . It is amazing how these things seem to fall into a pattern."
> "It is perhaps natural, Dada," I said, "It just shows how like each other we must be." (262)

Another such incident occurs in the tiger room. The novel begins and ends in the same room of the palace — the room with no chairs. Fifty-eight tiger skins had been sewn together to make a rug that covered the room from wall to wall. In the first scene the Maharaja of Begwad is the absolute ruler and Abhay, the heir apparent, not quite eighteen years old. They appear totally unlike, a study in contrasts. The father is old, reactionary, and taboo-ridden; the son is young, progressive, and rational. In the last scene, on the other hand, ten years and three hundred and thirty pages later, the Maharaja is dead and Abhay has abdicated his title after only forty-nine days as ruler; the state of Begwad has vanished into the totality of India. But Abhay is still sitting in the very same room with the tiger rug, leaning against the bolster his father had leaned against in the very first scene and where he declared: " 'No matter what anyone tells you, there will always be a Begwad and there will always be a Bedar as its ruler, so long as the sun and moon go round' " (19). In the last scene Abhay is alone, listening to the news of his own abdication: "The Maharaja of Begwad, His Highness Abhayraj Bedar the third, has communicated to the Government his decision to abdicate his title and renounce his privileges as the ex-ruling Prince . . . (245).

*The Princes* acquires an ironical dimension and a beautiful circularity from these incidents in the same room. Abhay has abdicated and returned to the very same place in the room from which he ran out in the first chapter, protesting against his father as a young man. The readers, too, are back in the very place where they started. Abhay's initiation is complete; he succeeds briefly to the title of his father, abdicates and becomes the spokesman for his father's values. He says, " . . . I myself went a long way towards sharing his views and values as far as our state was concerned" (20).

One other point regarding an important technical aspect of *The Princes* merits special consideration: the revelation of a complex and fluid personality through the searching use of the first-person point of view. Few writers have used the first person point of view to greater advantage than Malgonkar. Like Lt. Henry in *A Farewell to Arms,* Abhay, the first-person narrator, is the central figure in *The Princes;* not only has he played a role in the past events, but he even plays a crucial role in the very act of telling of those events. He is seen both as an actor and as a narrator, describing his experiences in retrospect but "in character." It is through his eyes that we see the events of *The Princes;* and it is through his developing consciousness that we are made to feel the impact of those events.

The masterstroke in the design of *The Princes,* then, is the self-characterization of Abhay, the narrator. The pattern of his speech and actions is so arranged as to bring about development of his character. Throughout the six stages of his evolution we get the im: pression of a dualism of the capital "I": he both narrates and experiences, is both young and old with a "here and now" dimension and a "then and there" dimension, is both "Abhay as I am now" and "Abhay as I was then." Malgonkar establishes a dual perspective or double vision as the narrating "I" looks back at his former self, the experiencing "I." Sometimes we are with Abhay, the uninitated youth, as in that scene of his open revolt against his father with which the novel opens. We are taken both closer and farther from the scene, closer to the eighteen-year-old, young Abhay and farther from him, but with the older (over thirty years old) Abhay, the narrator. On the one hand, we are on the plane of action, immersed in the reality of Abhay's character; we look out of him. On the other hand, we move by degrees away from him and push him into the past. We watch him as he was. The scene has a certain multidimensional quality with its continual implication of two minds. We realize with Abhay that life is lived forward but understood backward. Malgonkar has varied his point of view sufficiently to give us not only the psychological closeness to the subjective world of the younger Abhay, but also a psychological distance to prevent us from being fully immersed in the life of the younger Abhay. This juxtaposition of the two points of view creates a tension between the two poles of adulthood and youth, thus intensifying the theme of initiation. We get the impression of a complex, growing, and fluid personality as it encounters experience, a personality as it is defined in the interpenetration of its past and present self-awareness:

> Until I returned from war service, I used to squirm with shame at the thought of my father's private life. I now realize that, obsessed with the narrowness and naive values of youth, I judged him harshly, as indeed most of his world seems to have judged him. It was the war that helped me to grow up and to broaden my vision, the war and also the sudden explosion of the urges of my own body; and then I acquired what I like to think is a civilized tolerance for human frailties, learnt to tear my mind away from the petty and often false loyalties of childhood and youth.
>
> In those days I used to side with the world in condemning my father's infatuation, first with Bibi-bai and then with Amina and later still with Sherawathi, the South Indian girl. . . . At the time I could not understand how any man in his senses could have preferred another woman to my

mother who, I think, was one of the most beautiful women of her times. . . .
And my father's open preference for them was a continued torment to me.
Now of course I can understand how even the loveliest of women can make
themselves hateful to men;. . . . (55 - 57)

We see, then, that *The Princes* is a series of variations on the very
ancient theme of initiation. The concept of the initiation story,
clearly defined and applied with sensitivity, assists in a thorough understanding of the novel. Following the general pattern of myth with
some peculiar variations, Malgonkar has succeeded best in por-
traying Abhay's initiation which Ihab Hassan in *Radical Innocence*
(1961) has defined as "the first existential ordeal, crisis, or encounter
with experience in the life of a youth . . . a process leading through
right action and consecrated knowledge to a viable mode of life in the
world."[10]

### III   *Rhythm in* The Princes

In reading an Indian novel in English Western readers take immediate pleasure in the objective reporting of sounds and smells, of
exotic manners, foods, speech, and of the total atmosphere of India.
They take a secondary pleasure in the characterization — in
characters that convey Indian modes of thought and ways of life. But
there is a third and more important pleasure reserved for study — the
meaning conveyed by the "rhythm" and interplay of images. An
attempt to interpret an Indian novel solely on the basis of its
"rhythm" — a risky undertaking — would have the greatest chance
of success with *The Princes*. In *The Princes* not only do the various
"rhythms" of phrases, characters, incidents, and symbols offer clues
to what Malgonkar sought to represent, but the distribution of the
rhythms and symbols, their interrelation and their significance for
the illumination of certain themes and trends of the action, also help
us to a better insight into the meaning of the novel. The rhythm here
seems to be fully integrated into the structure of the novel and for
that reason seems to play a more meaningful role than in other Indian novels which largely depend for their success in the West on
their concentration upon the exotic at the expense of the novel's more
serious formalistic concerns. This explains why modern critics with
their specialized interest in structure and texture of novels have paid
little attention to the Indian novels. It is my present purpose to in-
vestigate some of the aspects of the rhythm in *The Princes*.

E. M. Forster in a provocative book titled *Aspects of the Novel* attributes to pattern and rhythm the potential for extending the significance of a literary work. The rhythm, he writes, is "not to be there all the time like a pattern, but by its lovely waxing and waning to fill us with surprise and freshness and hope."[11] He was the first to notice that recurrent incidents and images play a part in raising, developing, sustaining, and repeating emotion in a novel, which is somewhat analogous to the action of a recurrent theme or "motif" in a musical fugue or sonata, or in one of Wagner's operas. Forster creates an analogy between literature and music and calls to mind Beethoven's Fifth Symphony. In performance "the opening movement, the andante, and the trio-scherzi-trio-finale-trio-finale," must of necessity be played in sequence. Regardless of this, Forster claims, when the presentation is concluded, the listener can hear "something that has never actually been played."[12] The listener can hear, or experience within the symphony in total, the symphony as a "common entity." The possibility of this mental abstraction is rooted in rhythm. Forster asks if the same phenomenon might not occur in the area of literature. Is it possible that in the process of reading, movements, chords, crescendos, melodies might begin "to sound behind us, and . . . finally lead a larger existence than was possible at the time?"[13]

E. K. Brown developed Forster's idea further in his book *Rhythm in the Novel*. He defines the rhythmic process as "the combination of the repeated and the variable with the repeated as the ruling factor."[14] He discusses not only the simple kinds of "repetition with variation" that are combinations of word and phrase, sequences of incident and groupings of character but also a more complex combination — "the growth of a symbol as it accretes meaning from a succession of contexts."[15]

All these kinds of rhythm can be demonstrated in *The Princes*. No one has sought to explain just what makes it so powerful and moving, what gives one the feeling that it is more than a superb story of a Maharaja and of the splendor, pomp, and pageantry of his princely state of Begwad in India before independence. The source of this power can be discerned if we see that beneath its surface it is full of simple and complex rhythms, the varied kinds of repetition with variation that give to the novel an internal order and an expansion of meaning.

It will be convenient to begin with the simplest kind of rhythmic repetition in *The Princes* — the word-for-word repetition uncomplicated by the least variation. A novelist who writes at such great length as Malgonkar (*The Princes* is three hundred and forty-six pages long) cannot afford to say a thing only once. He is more or less forced to repeat a piece of information at least once if it has any significance. Often Malgonkar is not content with merely saying a thing twice. How often are we told that the princes were meant to go on for all time, so long as the sun and the moon themselves went round? That what we are given in life are cards dealt out by other hands? That princely life was very much like acting in a play? The statements are repeated two, three, and four times even, aiding the reader's memory and facilitating reading. It is the novelist's concession to his readers, recognizing the fact that the novel is long and the reader's memory short.

No one can fail to notice these repetitions. Let us consider the examples of the last paragraph in detail. The statement about the sun and the moon appears first in the title of chapter 1; it is then remembered by the narrator; and again we come across it in the Maharaja's pronouncement (13). Years later the narrator repeats it when he realizes that the years have given the lie to his father's statement (24). The sun and the moon continue to go round but the Maharaja and Begwad were no more.

Early in the novel the "cards" are so casually introduced that we hardly notice it:

Sometimes I wonder how different our lives would have been, both his and mine, if Kanakchand had never asked me to write his essay or if I had declined to do so. But then I have come to accept that these are ordained, that what we are given in life are cards dealt out by other hands. You could not deal out the cards yourself. (70)

A few years later Abhay goes to the Princes' College at Agra where Mr. Walter Ludlow, the headmaster, became an important influence in his life. Now the "cards" recur in another context:

"We have all come here with dealt out hands," the Head would say. "And some of us may be holding better cards than the others. I don't care as much about whether you play your cards well or badly as about whether you play them honourably. This is what you are going to be taught here." (78 - 79)

A few more years roll by and the princes including Abhay are now out of school and have become mere titled nonentities, living on pensions. Abhay recalls the days when they were true princes, the very salt of the earth:

I now realize that they represented a way of life that was already dying. We had a clean, carefree time, sheltered from the outside world. Like birds in antiseptic cages playing their own games. Perhaps if I had been more diligent in my studies, I would have got much more out of them than I did, and possibly even have prevented myself from making such a hash of my life. All I can say is that I took the cards as they were dealt out and played my hand as best I could, without trying to peep at the other man's cards. (80)

Malgonkar manages a most moving effect in which our memories of the school life of the narrator jostle with our impressions of the page in front of us.

For examples of verbal repetition complicated and enriched by variation we should turn again to the remarkable first scene in which Abhay sits face to face with his father. Consider the use of the word "play":

I could not help feeling that we were both acting in a play . . . it was seven-thirty, and as though at a signal, almost as though to heighten the illusion we were acting in a play and surrounded by stage props, two servants carried in brass bowls containing burning incense. . . .
   "This is so like a play," I remarked
   "What is?"
   "All this, us."
My father smiled. "All life is a play." he said. "All the world's a stage, all the men and women merely players." Have you done *As You Like It?"* (15)

Abhay thinks of the "play" again during the last days of his rule. His father had committed suicide because he had made up his mind not to sign the document of merger. Abhay became the ruler of Begwad for exactly forty-nine days. His wife Kamala, the new Maharani, did not want to go away from Begwad with the children at the time of the inauguration of the new administration. She felt she was running away, leaving her husband alone to face things. In the end Abhay persuaded her to go away with the children. Three days before the Durbar, he drove his family to the station:

There was a lump in my throat as the train moved away, carrying my son and my daughter waving wildly, and my wife poised, smiling and dignified and tearless — a Maharani conscious of the need for keeping up appearances. . . . As I stood looking at the departing train, I had a feeling that the play was coming to an end, and I was aware of the dramatic neatness of the ending. I was eager for the last three days to pass, for the end to be clean and swift. (319)

The day of the Durbar again reminds Abhay of the "play." The Bhils of Bulwara, the ignorant tribal people, docile as lambs, sat through the ceremony with Abhay and thirteen other rulers, who at one time thought of themselves as "lions." Kanakchand, an untouchable who is now a minister in the new administration, makes a venomous speech.

I was only half listening to the speech. Already I felt separated from the present. Whatever was happening had nothing to do with me. The play was already over, and this was nothing but a gathering of all the actors for a final curtain call. I and the other thirteen rulers who were present belonged to the dead, like ghosts hovering over the scene of their past. . . . They were only waiting for the show to be over, as though for release. (328)

There are many more instances of verbal repetition by which the different parts of the novel are linked up with one another. The word "squeal," for instance, is first used by the Maharaja in the first scene: " 'Sometimes you talk almost like an agitator yourself. . . . Almost like that boy I horsewhipped — the one with the mean little face. What was his name? Oh, yes, Kanakchand. Kanakchand the dhor, the untouchable. Remember how he squealed?' " (16).

Nearly ten years later when the novel is about to close, the word "squeal" returns. The Maharaja, Abhay, and Kanakchand live ten years of their lives before us. Kanakchand, now a cabinet minister, is horsewhipped again almost in the same place in the school:

Over the dimness that separated us, Kanakchand glowered in my direction in angry defiance, but there was also a quivering, frightened look on his face. He still cannot take it, I said to myself. He was one of those who would always squeal, one of those unfortunates who had not learned to take their punishment without showing it. (344)

"Squeal" occurs twice in between these two scenes. First, it occurs in the first horsewhipping scene. Abhay watches his schoolmate Kanakchand being horsewhipped by his father and wishes that he would stop moaning, that he would stand up erect and defiant and soundless. "But he cowered and whined. No one could have told him about lions and lambs and how important it was to take one's punishment without squealing" (73). And second, it recurs when Abhay was shocked and outraged to hear that his own dear mother married his hated enemy Abdulla Jan and was planning to go to Pakistan, the new country. She had changed her religion too and become a Muslim.

> There was a soft buzzing in my head, and somewhere at the back a nerve pounded as though it were going to burst. Why was I being given this extra punishment? Was this my reward for venerating the father-image I had created in my mind out of a man . . . who made a fetish of manliness, teaching me never to break down under punishment, never to squeal. . . . (323)

Another statement of his father echoes through the book. His father did not accept the Instrument of Accession that the nationalists had drawn up, nor their assurances: " 'They have always hated us. The vengeance of sheep can be a terrible thing' " (264). Later in the novel when Kanakchand humiliated the Maharaja, Abhay says: "He was humiliating someone who still held that he had no equal among men. That, truly, was the vengeance of sheep, as my father had said" (301). We are told still later by his wife that Abhay mumbled something like "the vengeance of the sheep can be a terrible thing" in his sleep during the last days of his rule.

A careful reader will not miss other recurrent words and phrases that Malgonkar has skillfully planted to raise and sustain emotion, to provide atmosphere, and to emphasize his theme. We are told more than once that the princes "were like ripe mangoes in late May, all ready to fall" (246, 248); that the "white cloth" between the Maharaja and his son was still white and spotless (222, 224, 225); that the Maharaja quoted the words of the Gita, "I am rich and wellborn, who else is equal to me?" (296, 300, 301, 302, 303); that Abhay swore to whip Kanakchand (268, 278, 301, 318, 345); and that Kanakchand scrambled around the dustbin (276, 289).

Another variety of rhythm, and one which is more complex and more effective than simple verbal artifices, is that offered by the grouping or arrangement of characters. It is a device through which a novelist duplicates characters. He may make similar people handle dissimilar problems or dissimilar people handle similar problems. In both cases repetition with limited variation is the dominant device. Malgonkar uses this repetitive device and shows the Maharaja and his son Abhay going through similar conventional Hindu arranged marriages, family alliances brought about by the pundits matching horoscopes. The Maharaja's was a failure; his wife deserted him. Abhay's, on the other hand, turned out to be a happy one; he loved his wife Kamala and they had two children. Another example of this rhythmic process is the custom of presenting the princes with concubines. The Maharaja was presented with his first concubine, Bibibai, on his sixteenth birthday. He accepted her, remained under her spell for years and later took two more concubines, Amina and Sherawathi. Abhay, on the other hand, sent his concubine, Zarina, away when he was presented with her, but he later accepted her.

As we have seen earlier, the Maharaja and Abhay are a study in contrasts. The father is old, reactionary, and taboo-ridden and rules Begwad for forty-nine years. The son is young, progressive, and rational and rules Begwad for forty-nine days. Episodes in their lives like those of marriage and concubinage are rhythmic or parallel in the sense that the form of the episode is the same in each and yet antithetical and offering contrast in the sense that one episode presents us with one kind of reality, one set of values, and the other presents us with a different kind of reality, a different set of values.

And yet, as the main action of the novel proceeds, the reader is struck not with the differences between them but with the similarities. As we have seen, as the son grows older he takes on more and more the traits of his father. Frequently these similarities, too, take the form of parallelism. Take for example their visits to the fort of Patalpat where the Jamdar-Khana, the family treasure, was hidden. As we noted earlier the treasure of the Bedars had been put together as the result of five generations of plunder; yet they could carry away only one article at each visit. When Abhay visited this secret place he picked up a wheel-lock pistol from its velvet case and brought it out: "The butt fitted snugly in my hand as though it had been made for me, and the barrel was almost weightless, so perfectly balanced it was." (258). Later in the novel Abhay learns that it was one of a pair. His father had brought out its twin when he had visited the Jamdar-Khana as a young man.

A yet more complex type of rhythm is that offered by a sequence of repeated incidents. For example the tiger room and the horsewhipping incidents. Malgonkar employs this device of repeated incidents to shape his plot. The novel acquires a beautiful circularity from these incidents placed at the beginning and repeated at the end. As we noted earlier the novel begins and ends in the same room in the palace — the room with no chairs. Fifty-eight tiger skins had been sewn together to make a rug that covered the room from wall to wall. In the first scene the Maharaja of Begwad is the absolute ruler and

Abhay the heir apparent. They appear totally unlike. The year is 1938. In the last scene on the other hand, nearly ten years later, the Maharaja is dead and gone, Begwad has vanished into the totality of India; Abhay has abdicated his title after forty-nine days of being the Maharaja. But Abhay is sitting in the same room with the tiger rug, leaning against the same bolster against which his father had leaned in the first scene. His father had declared then: " 'No matter what anyone tells you, there will always be a Bedar as its ruler, so long as the sun and the moon go round' " (19). Abhay in the last scene is alone and listening to the evening news of his own abdication: " 'The Maharaja of Begwad, His Highness Abhayraj Bedar the third, has communicated to the Government his decision to abdicate his title and renounce his privileges as an ex-Ruling Prince . . .' " (345). The scene is charged with irony.

The irony and the circularity are the more striking and satisfying because of the likeness between Abhay in the last scene and the Maharaja in the first. Abhay at the end is exactly the same in impulse as his father had been nearly ten years before. No one would have noticed the shift if he had changed places with the elder Maharaja. The son is a prolongation of his father. Abhay himself is fully aware of this likeness:

I myself went a long way towards sharing his views and values as far as our state was concerned. Indeed it seems to me that with the passing of years, I have come to identify myself more and more with those values, with the result that today I feel myself a spokesman for whatever the princely order once stood for.

"Maharaja Abhayraj proved to be just as much of a reactionary as his father," the Settlements Minister wrote in his memoirs. He was referring to me, of course, and instead of feeling resentful, I was elated by the rebuke, proud of being thought like my father. (20)

Malgonkar enforces this theme of the likeness between the two princes by repeating the substance of the scene of horsewhipping of Kanakchand. As we noted earlier, in the first of the incidents the Maharaja whipped Kanakchand, a poor untouchable student, for cheating and for wearing the white cap of the nationalists at the Asokraj High School. More than ten years later in a scene set very near the end of the novel Abhay whips with a riding crop the same Kanakchand, now a minister in the new administration at the same

school which is now called The New National High School.
Malgonkar manages a moving effect in which our memories of the
first incident mingle with our impressions of the second.

There are many more repeated incidents in the novel — the visits
of the elder and of the younger prince to the Bhils of Bulwara (91 -
95; 312), the elder prince's habit of shooting copper coins in the air
(98, 267, 307), and the Holland-gun incident. Malgonkar's use of the
device avoids the stiffening of repetition into mere formula. The
repetitive incidents not only suggest a sense of immutable order but
also help the reader in linking up different parts of the novel. They in-
tensify the unity of the novel.

The special world of *The Princes* is not the best of all possible
worlds. The animals, birds, and fishes which inhabit it are tigers,
lions, crocodiles, snakes, owls, pigs, dogs, fireflies, crows, lambs, and
oysters which seen individually do not seem to be important but in
their totality contribute to the tone and atmosphere of the novel:
("all of us were exposed to the harsh glare of the sun like frogs under
an overturned slab. . . ."). Of these, the tigers, lambs, and oysters
which are used with great power and beauty, become "expanding
symbols." This brings me to a last type of rhythm present in the
novel. This type of rhythm, like the others we have considered, is the
modern equivalent of the classical unities, having all the classical ad-
vantages and none of their severe limitations. An expanding symbol
is a symbol in which the meaning is enriched and enlarged each time
it recurs. Its recurrence — the number of times and frequency with
which it recurs — suggests both its rhythm and its growth.

The tiger is one of the grand controlling images and presences in
*The Princes*. Malgonkar skillfully employs the device of incremental
repetition to suggest many associations common to the tiger. In its
multiple determinations the tiger stands for the wild animal, for
status, for princely power, and for that mysterious force — "divine
instrument" — that intervenes in human affairs. The aura of implications and associations which surrounds many of the scenes of
tiger hunting is complex enough to delight the purest or most
ambiguity-loving disciples of William Empson, who treats this theme
in his book *Seven Types of Ambiguity*. Begwad, consisting mainly of
hills and jungles, had always been renowned as the tiger land of India. It was a minor state with no education or industry to speak of,
and its ruler received only a seventeen-gun salute. Yet it had become
recognized as one of the best states for shooting tigers, and its ruler
as one of the best organizers of tiger hunts. Every year the Maharaja
played host to at least two or three important visitors from England.

The Maharaja, who had shot his eightieth tiger on his fortieth birthday, was an outstanding marksman. He and his shikar officer,
Hanuman Singh, had an elaborate organization and had reduced the
business of finding tigers to an almost infallible science. Even the
visitors who missed their first shots managed to bag their tigers after
all. It was the tigers that gave status to Begwad and its Maharaja.
The ruler owed his social recognition among the British and among
other princes to his ability to produce a tiger:

Gwalior could feed five hundred guests on gold plate; Indore had French
cooks . . . Jaipur had its polo, Kolhapur its cheetah hunt . . . other states had
their dancing girls, temples, cave paintings. Begwad just had to have some
distinctive feature of its own.
    "If it weren't for our tigers, we would never have any visitors at all," my
father used to explain. "That is the only thing that we can give them that the
other princes cannot: a tiger. Dammit, even the Viceroy had said that I can
guarantee a tiger." (113)

The tiger was more than a status symbol. We have seen how two
important scenes of the novel are set in a room with a tiger rug which
covered the room from wall to wall. The Maharaja, who often gives
the impression of riding a tiger, speaks of events as having taken
place before or after he shot a particular tiger. He tells with a special
glint in his eyes that the Bihar earthquake had occurred just the day
after he had shot the Ambewadi man-eater, or that King Edward
VIII had abdicated during the week he was trying to bag the
Palapani tigress. Tigers were the major landmarks of his life. He had
shot ninety-nine tigers, and his great ambition was to shoot his hundredth tiger before his fiftieth birthday and thus to get his name in
Rowland Ward's book of records. He and Hanuman Singh had
followed with special interest the activities of the Kolaras tiger,
which became one of the characters. When the Maharaja realized
that his rule as a tiger of a prince was nearly over, he says:

"I am in my fiftieth year — must shoot my hundredth tiger. . . . Don't you
see, Abhay, that we are all going to be finished off soon? We might as well
spread whatever time is left to us in doing the things we enjoy. . . . What I
should like to do is to shoot the Kolaras giant. . . . Everything is already over.
. . . (273)

In the last and most dramatic tiger hunt of the book — *The
Princes* has many marvelously detailed descriptions of the drama of
the tiger hunt — the Maharaja shot the Kolaras giant but did not

succeed in killing him. The general rules were that a wounded tiger had to be tracked and finished off after giving it half an hour. It was the privilege of the host, the Maharaja, to go after all wounded tigers. He had always gone after wounded tigers alone, and he had always managed to get them, but this time when he went after the Kolaras giant, alone, refusing to take Abhay or Hanuman Singh with him, he had made up his mind not to kill but be killed by the Kolaras tiger. The wounded Kolaras tiger and the Maharaja met their death together:

I did not want anyone other than Hanuman Singh to know that the Maharaja of Begwad had committed suicide because he had made up his mind not to sign the document of merger. . . . We did not measure the tiger. I did not want him to be stretched and pulled about and humbled, his pink deskinned carcass left for a feast of vultures. In my mind he was no longer a tiger but something of a divine instrument sent to aid my father in his hour of need, something that had made it possible for him to realize his wish that he would not live to see the end, made it possible, too, for him to die in the way he would have wished. I gave instructions for the tiger to be cremated where he lay, in a high pile of sandlewood. The giant of Kolaras did not go into a book of records, but he had suddenly become something of a god. (309 - 10)

Malgonkar uses the tiger as an expanding symbol to suggest by association more than it signifies. The recurrence of the tiger and the Maharaja's powerful attraction to it suggest that they were alike. The association between the Maharaja and the tiger adds to our feeling of how remarkable and how strong they were. It can be said of the tiger, as E.M. Forster said of Vinteuil's music, that it has a life of its own, that it is almost an actor in the drama. Malgonkar skillfully uses the tiger with its extraordinary suggestiveness to capture and render that part of life that is elusive, mysterious, and unknown. We appear to be in the presence of something so elusive that we cannot understand it. The tiger accretes meaning in a slow uneven way from the succession of contexts in which it occurs. By this means Malgonkar takes us beyond the conventional elements of the novel — the story, the characters, and the settings — and reveals something of his meaning, not in perfect clarity, but in a sequence of sudden flashes. He is struggling to communicate an idea, an emotion which can only be glimpsed, never fully seen.

Two other expanding symbols, much less pervasive and much less complicated than the tiger but equally striking, are the lambs and the oysters which recur in a variety of contexts. The lambs are contrasted with the tigers early in the novel, and the father is contrasted with the son. When Abhay was eleven years old, he became so angry with his father over the death of his pet lamb called Cannonball that he even wanted to kill him. Seeing him weeping over its death in a contest, the Maharaja admonished him and then made him eat its eyes and drink whisky without breaking down in public:" 'We are like lions, we do not weep for dead lambs. . . . It is important not to squeal, to show hurt. Be a man my son' " (33). Abhay emerged from this harsh initiation with a sense of triumph. Seven years later when Abhay was eighteen years old another dispute took place between him and his father. It was over his father's reactionary attitudes to the nationalists. The lambs occur in a new context. "Something in the way my father was staring at me made me stop. 'It is surprising how quickly the horns grow on the foreheads of lambs,' he remarked" (17). Kanakchand is a "lamb" because he did not know how to handle his punishment without squealing (73; 344). In still another context, the Bhils of Bulwara were docile as "lambs" throughout the ceremony of Begwad's merger, which they could barely understand.

The "oysters" also develop rhythmically with all their associations of luxury, sensuality, and close-lipped uncommunicativeness. One of the princes who thought that the Instrument of Accession was nothing but an instrument of their destruction says that the princes were just like "the oysters invited to attend the tea party of the Walrus and the Carpenter" (265). At the historic last session of the full Chamber of the Princes, to Abhay in the gallery, the princes who sat in rows looked like "oysters arranged on a salver, some fat and plump, some old, . . ." (265). Yet a few pages later Abhay was irritated when his father quoted the oyster poem of Lewis Carroll. Levity was intolerable on a solemn occasion:

" 'But wait a bit the oysters cried.
Before we have our chat;
For some of us are out of breath,
and all of us are fat!
"Wait a bit that's all we can say. . . . How long will they give us before they send us another telegram saying: 'Now if you're ready, oysters dear, we can begin to feed.' " (280)

*The Princes,* then, is a complex work, coherent in structure, richly textured, and resonant with symbols and images. It is unified and given its shape and significance by a complex system of repetitions. Its greatness and complexity are dependent on Malgonkar's mastery

of repetitions of the sort examined here — of phrases, characters, incidents, and symbols — which with or without variations enforce his
themes and make them more emphatic in their resonance by means
of a network of implications and associations, and echoes that they
produce.

These are but a few of the things that can be said about *The
Princes,* a novel of many facets. They will perhaps suffice to call
attention to some aspects of Malgonkar's constructive art that have
commonly been left out of account even by those who have praised it
most highly.

## CHAPTER 5

# A Bend in the Ganges:
# Motifs of Initiation

IN some respects *A Bend in the Ganges* (1964) resembles *The Princes* (1963) — both novels deal with contemporary Indian history especially the decade between 1938 and 1948; both tell stories of young men especially their growth toward maturity and understanding of the world; and both suggest that an immense amount of research has gone into getting the facts straight.

There are, however, important differences. Whereas *The Princes* tells the story from the point of view of the ruling princes, *A Bend in the Ganges* tells the same story from the point of view neither of the ruling princes nor of the nonviolent Gandhian followers of the Congress Party but of the violent revolutionaries or terrorists who had no faith in the Gandhian technique of nonviolence. *The Princes* deals with the education of a prince — Abhay — but *A Bend in the Ganges* is concerned with the education of three troubled and angry young men drawn from the middle class — Gian Talwar, Debi-dayal, and Shafi Usman, two Hindus, and one Muslim who were members of a terrorist group called "The Freedom Fighters." Debi and Shafi die in the terrible upheaval that followed the Indian independence day. Gian, on the other hand, emerges from the violent upheaval chastened, maturer, and wiser in the ways of the world. Above all else, *A Bend in the Ganges* is preoccupied with Gian's growth toward self-knowledge and understanding of the world. It is his growth that is the central action of the novel. He grows before our eyes from a naive and impulsive young man in the first scene who throws his dark-blue and yellow football blazer into the fire to become a convert of Gandhi's nonviolence to a decisive and mature adult in the driver's seat who in the last scene starts the engine and leaps forward with the convoy. There is something more profound at work than a simple story of murder and revenge or contemporary Indian history — something that offers a way to approach the novel. Gian Talwar, the

"Initiation" hero, passes through a series of ordeals to achieve social and moral maturity.

Perhaps a brief outline of the story may help bring these notions into sharper focus. The story begins with Mahatma Gandhi in the market square, seated on the dais, his right hand twirling a brass spinning wheel, his left feeding it with candles of cotton wool. It is a Monday, his day of silence. There is a fire in front of him into which a group of people standing around are throwing British garments. Gian Talwar, a young college student, almost without knowing it, throws his prized dark-blue and yellow football blazer, made of imported English material, into the fire and finds himself repeating the slogan "Mahatma Gandhi-Ki Jai, Victory to Nonviolence." Thus begins Gian's brief career as a disciple of Gandhi, who had a hypnotic effect on him.

Gian goes to Duriabad for college study from a village called Konshet. At college he makes friends with Debi-dayal, the only son of Dewan Bahadur Tekchand Kerwad, the owner of the Kerwad Construction Company. Debi belongs to a terrorist group called The Freedom Fighters who believe that "nonviolence is the philosophy of sheep." The Freedom Fighters pride themselves on being the most successful group of terrorists, with an impressive record of achievement. Their leader, Shafi Usman, a young Muslim, was the most wanted man in the state. They were all fervent patriots, dedicated to the overthrow of British rule in India and to Hindu-Muslim-Sikh unity. This was a time when sharp differences were arising between the Hindus and the Muslims. The Freedom Fighters were cutting telephone wires and removing fishplates from railway tracks. It is when they blow up an Air Force plane with some explosives stolen from the Kerwad Construction Company that they get into trouble. Debi-dayal and Shafi are involved in this particular act of sabotage. Shafi escapes but Debi-dayal is arrested, tried, sentenced to life imprisonment, and finally sent to the Andamans, the penal colony.

Meanwhile, Gian gets involved with a family feud, renounces nonviolence because of a series of reprisals taken by the Big House toward his family over the marriage of his grandfather to a lower caste woman, and murders Vishnu-dutt, a member of his family. He, too, is imprisoned, tried, sentenced to life imprisonment, and finally transported to the Andamans. Here he meets Debi-dayal who continues to hate the British. Gian, on the other hand, works on the Pro-British side and has no scruples even in cooperating with Patrick Mulligan, a British official of the Cellular Jail. Gian, acting as "administrative spy," betrays Debi-dayal, who is flogged for trying to escape. When the second World War reaches the Andamans and the Japanese arrive, Gian escapes to India.

Debi-dayal does not run away; he cooperates with "the Japanese brothers," the new masters of the Andamans. With the help of Colonel Yamaki, the commanding officer, Debi makes plans to go to India to work from behind the enemy lines — to blow up bridges, sink ships, and burn down planes. Within a week he is on board a destroyer on the way to India. The Japanese escort him right into Kohima, in Northwestern Assam, where he joins the swarms of refugees.

Back in India Gian lies to Tekchand and Sundari about his friendly relationship with Debi-dayal in the Andamans and succeeds in getting a job as shipment supervisor in Bombay for Kerwad Construction Company. Sundari who feels attracted to him meets Gian often in Bombay. But when Debi-dayal tells her that Gian had lied to her she becomes angry and speaks harshly to him: That is what you were to me — a male whore; that is what your great love has meant for me (317).

In Lahore Debi-dayal confronts Shafi Usman, hits him, and in revenge takes away his girl, Mumtaz. In Bombay Sundari and Debi plan to let their parents know of Debi's return to India and of his marriage with Mumtaz. Sundari undertakes to go to Duriabad to prepare their parents' minds to accept Mumtaz as their daughter-in-law. Debi and Mumtaz were to follow her four days later. Meanwhile, the communal riots flare up in the Panjab. Trains are attacked and all railway services come to a stop. There seems no possibility of Debi's making the journey to Duriabad. The year is 1947: "The year of one of the bloodiest upheavals of history: seventeen million people had to flee, leaving their homes; nearly half a million were killed; over a hundred thousand women, young, and old, were abducted, raped, mutilated" (viii).

Sundari and her parents are in Duriabad in Pakistan where mass migrations begin. The riots and migrations were occasioned by the cutting up of the country. The Hindus were fleeing to India and the Muslims were fleeing to Pakistan. Mr. and Mrs. Tekchand and Sundari wish to join the convoy to India when the whole of the Panjab is caught up in the blaze of hatred. There is in effect a civil war. It is at this time that Gian, Shafi, and Debi-dayal make their separate journeys to Duriabad. Gian and Shafi meet and clash at the home of the Tekchands. In a violent episode Shafi kills Mrs. Tekchand, and

Sundari kills Shafi beating his head with the shiva image. Gian helps Sundari to reach freedom and safety in India. Mr. Tekchand is swept away by the storm of violence. Debi-dayal who is on his way to Duriabad is killed by an angry mob. As he lay on the ground, his clothes torn, the sun rises in the land of the five rivers on the day of freedom — August 15, 1947.

As one can see from this synopsis, Malgonkar relates not one tale, but three interlocking tales. First, the story of Gian's growth toward moral maturity. Second, how Debi-dayal, the terrorist, withdraws gradually from the political life of the country into the life of domestic happiness with Mumtaz. And third, how Shafi, the idealistic leader of the Freedom Fighters, becomes transformed into a fanatical hater of the Hindus. All three stories are about the growth of troubled and angry young men — two Hindus and one Muslim — during a troubled and violent period just before and after Independence Day in India. Above all else, the novel is a study in growth whether that growth be Gian's or Debi's or Shafi's. Debi and Shafi die in the middle of the process of their growth. Gian alone survives and continues to grow.

The novel has another theme: nobody is exempt from the capacity for violence. Gandhi, the great apostle of nonviolence, might appear in the opening scene to convert Gian Talwar to his creed of nonviolence but the theme that runs through the novel from beginning to end is man's hidden capacity for violence often brought out by the destructive acts of others. It is a novel with three different stories skillfully interwoven, and all three work out the theme of violence, repeating it again and again. Gian kills Vishnu-dutt who had earlier murdered Hari, Gian's brother. Later in the Andamans Gian even beheads Ramoshi's corpse to obtain gold. Debi-dayal destroys a British plane. Shafi shoots down Debi's mother. Even the lovely Sundari is guilty of violence — she breaks Shafi's skull with a statue of Shiva. There are also others, unnamed, caught up in the holocaust — large masses of people, Hindus and Muslims alike, committing numberless acts of violence. Debi-dayal and Shafi themselves become victims of violence. Only Gian and Sundari survive the violence at the end of the novel. Everyone else kills or gets killed.

It must be said, then, that *A Bend in the Ganges* is essentially a study in Gian's growth and his capacity for violence. It is only by immersion in the flux of experience — in Konshet, in the Andamans and in Duriabad — that he becomes disciplined and develops in character, conscience, or soul. The novel depicts his self-combat; it probes his state of mind and analyzes his gradual transformation under the incessant pinpricks and bombardments of life. Gian's slow quest for personal development and his discovery of the nature of reality lie at the heart of the novel. Malgonkar takes Gian through three stages in his growth toward moral maturity. First, he is unable to distinguish between the heroic dreams of his commitment to Gandhian nonviolence and the harsh realities of his own nature and of the politics of India's struggle for freedom. Second, he goes through a period of confusion and doubt, of deceit and rationalization, as reality begins to intrude upon the falseness of his private dream world. And finally, he solves his problem when he abandons his search for comfortable justifications and learns to see the world in its true light.

As the novel opens, Gian is troubled by the conflict he vaguely senses between his heroic image of self and fleeting glimpses of harsh reality. As he takes off his dark-blue and yellow football blazer under the influence of Gandhi and pushes his way through the crowd toward the fire he feels a "sudden desire to turn back, to fight down his irrational impulse . . ." (5). But it is too late. He steps forward and flings the coat into the flames. "Mahtma Gandhi-Ki Jai!" Gian found himself muttering. 'Bharat-mata-ki Jai! The path of Ahimsa is not for cowards.' The words were almost like a private prayer" (6).

At college he wears Khaddar, the rough homespun which had become the uniform of the Indian National movement. He confidently declares to his friends, Debi-dayal, Shafi Usman, and others:

"I am a follower of Gandhi. . . . Gahdhiji is a God . . . only he can bring freedom to India . . . only the Mahatma can lead us to freedom, through the path of nonviolence. . . . No man has the right to raise his hand against another, whatever the provocation. I shall never do it. . . . Nonviolence is not for the weak. . . ." (13 - 15).

Yet when he saw his brother Hari and Vishunu-dutt quarrel, both their faces taut with rage, Gian "felt weak, and was trembling. . . . The sweat was running down his armpits, and his lips were gumming up for lack of moisture. . . ." (41).

Hari now sees Vishnu-dutt holding a long-handled timber axe in his hands and advises Gian not to follow him. But Gian pleads, his words almost choking in his throat, " 'But I want to be with you . . . whatever happens . . .' " (42).

Deep in his heart, we know from the narrator, Gian really does not want to get involved:

But he did not want to go on. He wishes to hang back, to run away. . . . This was not his fight; it was Hari's. . . . His was the path of nonviolence — the nonviolence of the strong, he reminded himself, arising from courage. . . .

But he did not feel courageous. "Let's both go back," he blurted out, almost in spite of himself. (42)

Gian does not follow Hari; he stood rooted to the ground, unable to move. Hari went into the hut where Vishnu-dutt mercilessly murdered him with the axe. Gian's knees tremble.

Hari's murder disturbs Gian's heroic image of self. Then follows a period of doubt and confusion as fleeting glimpses of reality intrude upon his private world. Malgonkar interprets the human situation in terms of the tensions created in the contrast between Gian as he idealizes himself in his inner thought and Gian as he actualizes himself in the stress of experience. The inflated man gradually gets deflated by collisions with reality. Gian's nonviolence crumbles the moment it meets a major test; even his nationalism begins to waver. He had "already begun to doubt whether India could ever do without the British. It was they who were so scrupulous about the ends of justice" (120). Gian also keeps accusing himself of being a coward: "Was that why he had embraced the philosophy of nonviolence without question — from physical cowardice, not from courage? Was his nonviolence merely that of the rabbit refusing to confront the hound?" (44).

Gian wants to see Vishnu-dutt hanged for Hari's murder. As the axe was not found Vishnu-dutt was acquitted. Gian, despising himself, makes a systematic search of a tank for the axe, finds it, goes directly to Vishnu-dutt and kills him with the same axe with which he had murdered his brother. At the trial that followed Gian was given a sentence of transportation for life. When Debi finds Gian in the Andamans many thoughts go through his mind:

Was Gian the man, Debi wondered, the nonviolent disciple of Gandhi who had been convicted for murder? He cursed and shook his head in disgust. Gian was certainly not the man. He was typical of the youth of India, vacillating, always seeking new anchors, new directions, devoid of any basic convictions. He had been dedicated, so he had told them, to truth and non-violence. He had already jettisoned nonviolence; how far would he go with truth? (147).

In the Andamans Prison Gian remains confused, and seeks solace in bold deceit and rationalization. When a letter from Sundari arrives for Debi-dayal with some hidden money he steals her photographs and money and hides them in the hollow of a jackfruit tree. As an administrative spy for Mulligan, he spies on other inmates of the prison, and even betrays Debi-dayal, and gets him flogged for attempting to escape from the Cellular Jail. Debi-dayal has nothing but contempt for Gian: "He was suspicious of Gian. He had heard him spouting truth and nonviolence . . . a man without principles, his nonviolence a cover for cowardice, for a total absence of patriotic fervour. Now he had shown himself to be one of those who played along with the authorities to win petty favours. . . ." (160). Later Debi was approached by Gian with a plan for escape. Debi says, " 'I would willingly rot in a cell here rather than associate with someone like you and become free. You are scum; you are far worse than Balbahadur because he at least is openly hostile — you spout truth and nonviolence. You are the sort of man through whom men like Mulligan rule our country . . .' " (187).

The real world continues to make inroads upon his false views and false self-estimate. Back in India under a false name — Maruti Rao — Gian sells some sovereigns which he had got after beheading the corpse of Ramoshi. In Duriabad he meets Debi-dayal's parents and sister and tells lies about his friendship with Debi-dayal in the Andamans. He even succeeds in getting a job at the Kerwad Construction Company in Bombay with a new name, Gian Joshi. Sundari has an affair with Gian even though she was married. But when Debi-dayal himself reaches India and tells all about Gian to Sundari in Bombay, she becomes aware of Gian's deceit and vainglorious image of himself. She becomes furious, exposes his lies and even calls him "a male whore." Gian has reached the bottom of his moral degradation.

In the end Gian is forced to abandon his pseudoheroic image of himself, his false views and comfortable justifications. Debi-dayal had called him "scum"; Sundari had called him "a male whore." These remarks and the experiences of August, 1947, help Gian toward a more objective estimate of himself. On August 15, 1947, India and Pakistan became independent nations. While most of India and Pakistan celebrated Independence Day, in the Panjab it was a day of violence and terror. Mobs of Hindus, Muslims, and Sikhs on both sides of the border, raped, slaughtered, and burned one another. The era of large scale massacres and mass migrations began. One of the bloodiest upheavals of history took place during those hectic months. In the sundered Panjab nearly five million people left their homes and crossed the border. Probably around 200,000 men, women, and children were killed. It is impossible to describe the fear, the heartbreak and the destitution which this unforeseen upheaval produced.

It is during this communal war of August in the Panjab that Gian undergoes a change; he experiences for the first time "unselfishness," accepts the world for what it is and emerges a triumphant victor over falseness. From Delhi he rushes to Duriabad on the other side of the border in order to rescue Sundari and her parents, without the slightest regard for his own safety. The Panjab upheaval represents life at its most intense flux, and, therefore, it exploits the greatest possible potentialities for change. Gian now can understand that he must lose his soul in order to save it. In the thick of reality, so to speak, he realized the value of unselfishness. He tells Sundari:

"Look . . . this is something you won't believe, but it happens to be the truth. I don't know what possessed you, that day of the explosion, to come and look for me. That is exactly the sort of thing I am doing now. I have just arrived from Delhi; it took me a whole week. And the things that are happening everywhere, there as well as here, are not such that your father and mother should be exposed to. It came to me all of a sudden, in the middle of the night, when I discovered that you people were still here. So I came, to give whatever help I can. . . ."

"How I wish I could believe in you, Mr. Talwar. You have never done anything without a selfish motive. You even professed to fall in love, with a mercenary motive; you sold my brother to secure favors. . . ."

"Since we are talking about my degradation, may I tell you that that is partly the reason why I have come?" Gian said. "To try and prove, if only to myself, that there can be some good in the weakest of human beings . . . and remember that I was not caught up on this side, as you say. I came." (338 - 39)

This surely is a new Gian Talwar — confident, mature, unselfish and liberated from his imprisoning ego. Gian's "smile, the assurance, the arrogant awareness of being in command made Sundari tremble" with anger. He refuses to go away. When Shafi and his friends attack the Kerwad House, Gian fights them boldly. Shafi and Sundari's mother died in the scuffle. Gian then gets Sundari into a car — her father had disappeared — sits in the driver's seat, starts the engine, and leaps forward to join the convoy to India. Gian has achieved, though somewhat slowly and painfully, a level of maturity and self-knowledge that he lacked in the beginning.

Malgonkar does not take Debi-dayal and Shafi Usman through all the stages of development. An initiation story usually reveals a young man's development through his experiences in many areas: his formal schooling, religion, sex, marriage, work, social relationships, and travel. Gian, as we have seen, develops into a full and harmonious personality progressing from innocence to knowledge. Debi-dayal and Shafi Usman, on the other hand, do not complete their apprenticeship for life; they died before their education is complete. Nevertheless, they do undergo changes. Something happens not only to them but also in them.

Debi-dayal joins The Freedom Fighters and becomes a terrorist because he was shocked to see a British soldier in the act of raping his mother. In the novel he moves from intense involvement in national politics and public life to a stage of indifference to political life and finally to withdrawal into domestic life with a wife. He embarks on his quest for development as a Freedom Fighter by eating with other Freedom Fighters, Hindùs, Muslims, and Sikhs alike, a simple meal of coarse bread and beef-and-pork curry, symbolizing the flouting of the sacred impositions of all the religions of India: Hinduism, Islam, and Sikhism. All Freedom Fighters were required to renounce vegetarianism and the taboos of religion. Their oath of initiation had to be signed in blood drawn from the little finger of the left hand. Debi-dayal destroys a British Air Force plane and so is transported to the Andamans. When the Japanese take over the Cellular Jail he cooperates with them, because he continues to hate the British rule.

It is when he returns to India that we begin to notice some changes in him; he is less actively involved in the politics of India even when hundreds of thousands of Indians are arrested during "Quit India" protests of 1942. In Assam, as assistant stockman at the Silent Hill Tea Garden, he assumes the name Kalu-ram and works without any political action or interest for nearly two years (271 - 72). He becomes disillusioned even about the Japanese, who barely two years earlier had seemed admirable.

And although it was not his, Debi-dayal's war, the prospect of an Anglo-American victory was somehow less abhorrent than that of a Japanese victory. He had seen the Japanese from too close to wish that their rule should replace that of the British in India. . . . Two years of softness, of introspection, of worrying about rights and wrongs, had only increased his uncertainty; for the rights and wrongs seemed to be still as hopelessly mixed up as ever. . . . (273 - 74).

In Lahore in order to hurt Shafi, Debi-dayal ran away with Mumtaz, Shafi's girl. Mumtaz takes care of him, looks after the house, cooking, washing, and sweeping. She dresses the wound on his hand, inflicted by Shafi. Gradually Debi-dayal grows more and more dependent on her; they begin to live like man and wife in a little cottage by the dairy farm.

Was this how people got involved? he asked himself. Three months earlier he could never have imagined having anything to do with a girl like Mumtaz, but now the thought of sending her away suddenly seemed callous. . . . Had he tied himself irrevocably down because he could not make a harsh decision? . . . He had become so used to having her there that suddenly it was difficult to think of life without her, despite her background . . . like the beggar in the fable who had acquired a cat to get rid of the mice in his hut, he had now become involved in the coils of what they called Sansar — the web of responsibility. You could not keep a cat without providing it with milk: that was the lesson of the fable. You had to keep a cow too, and then a servant to look after the cow, and so on.

He had now become a man with ties. From now on he would have to live as other men lived, doing humdrum jobs, wrapped up in domesticity, not allowing themselves to be distracted by political inequities. . . . (303 - 05).

This is what happened to Basu, another Freedom Fighter, who had withdrawn from public life; he, too, had drifted into domestic life.

Debi-dayal and Mumtaz, now completely indifferent to politics, plan to go to Duriabad in the Panjab, on the Pakistan side of the border. Debi-dayal was going into the family fold with his wife, to introduce her to his parents. But it was a terrible time — the middle of August, 1947 — to travel in the Panjab. There was unimaginable chaos; gangs of hooligans were patroling the streets, murdering and raping Hindus, Muslims, and Sikhs alike; all train services had been canceled. Nevertheless, Debi, under an assumed Muslim name, Karim, wants to take Mumtaz to his home in Duriabad. On their way to Duriabad an angry mob stopped the refugee train, discovered Debi-dayal to be a Hindu, and murdered him on the spot. He was killed on the day of independence — August 15, 1947. He had begun his life as a rebel with a passionate desire for Indian independence, but toward the end of his life he became disillusioned about politics and fond of quiet homelife. A stormy petrel is thus transformed into a tame householder in the stress of experience.

Shafi Usman's transformation is of a different sort. He is motivated to violence against the British because his father was the victim of the Jalianwalla Massacre of 1919. General Dyer had ordered his soldiers with machine guns to open fire on innocent people in the enclosure of the Jalianwalla bagh, and three hundred and seventy-nine people were killed and over a thousand people wounded. Shafi becomes the leader of the Freedom Fighters. He was born a Muslim but became a Sikh; his religion of Islam meant nothing to him. At a time when Hindus and Muslims were in opposite camps Shafi was the leader of a group in which Hindus, Muslims, and Sikhs worked together in perfect harmony. They were all young men, fervent patriots, dedicated not only to the overthrow of British rule but also to Hindu-Muslim-Sikh unity. As we have seen they ate beef-and-pork curry to symbolize their renunciation of vegetarianism and taboos of religion. Their secret mode of greeting, too, symbolized this unity — "Jai-ram!" was answered by "Jai-rahim!" The name of Rama was sacred to all Hindus, and that of Rahim, equally sacred to the Muslims. Shafi, the idealistic leader of this group, becomes transformed before our eyes into a fanatical hater of Hindus. He begins his life hating the Britishers but ends up hating Hindus.

Shafi's change begins imperceptibly after a talk with Hafiz Khan who directed the terrorist activities from Bombay. He was the acknowledged chief of the terrorists in India, just as Gandhi was the chief of the National Congress. One day Hafiz came to Shafi to speak to him alone. He speaks to Shafi in blunt terms: " 'We must now turn our back on the Hindus, otherwise we shall become their slaves. . . . The time has come to take a second look — to reorientate ourselves. The enemies of the moment are not the British; they are the Hindus. That's what we must recognize!' " (83).

Hafiz reads cuttings from *The Dawn* and *Trident* and the *Awaz* to prove that Hindus were enslaving and ill-treating Muslims. He wants Shafi to change his tactics and organize Muslims to carve out their own country without Hindu overlordship. At first Shafi was unconvinced and skeptical. But when he had to warn all Freedom Fighters that their meeting place was going to be raided he warned only Muslim members. The others were arrested and put into jail. Hafiz and the paper clippings probably had a lot to do with this decision of Shafi.

Shafi now begins to work in collaboration with Hafiz:

He had changed, almost inevitably, as the whole of India had changed. The fervour of youth had been tempered, its follies rectified . . . As far as Shafi was concerned . . . he had now become convinced there was no possibility

that the Hindus and Muslims could live together. The days of religious unity
. . . were gone. The Hindus had shown their hand. . . .

He shaves off his beard, and discards his turban, and with it goes the Kada
(steel bangle worn by the Sikhs), the Kirpan (sword)), and the Kangi (comb)
of the Sikh religion. "How absurd it had been," he kept telling himself, "going about as a Sikh, when one detested them even more than one did the Hindus." (282).

Now for Shafi and millions of other Muslims the fight was no
longer against the British, but against the Hindus who were aspiring
to rule over them. Shafi and his friends enter the Kerwad House in
Duriabad, insult and abuse Sundari and her parents. Shafi even
seized one of the statues of their Hindu Gods, and crashes it on
another. And, finally, he kills Sundari's mother in a frenzy. In a scuffle that follows Sundari hits him with a heavy statue of Shiva and
rains blows on his head again and again, until his skull cracks open
and blood and brains spurt out in a red and white mass.

*A Bend in the Ganges* does not merely tell the stories of young men
and women during a time of national ferment — of Gian, Sundari,
Debi-dayal, Mumtaz, Shafi, Basu, Gopal, Hari, and Malini. It could
also be regarded as a documentary narrative dealing with the violent
rather than nonviolent aspects of India's struggle for independence.
Gandhi appears only briefly in one chapter of the book. Malgonkar
gives the impression that he has investigated the circumstances of actual events in the Panjab during the religious war of 1947. Like John
Hershey's *Hiroshima* or Truman Capote's *In Cold Blood* or
Khushwant Singh's *Train to Pakistan* Malgonkar's novel is
recurrently and explicitly exact about events in relation to time; he
pays scrupulous attention to chronology. A glance at Appendix 2,
*India Before and After Independence,* will establish this point of
documentary authenticity. All characters except Gandhi are fictional
but the political situation and the events — Jalianwala Bagh, World
War II, the Japanese advance in the East, the Fall of Singapore, Quit
India, the Communal disturbances and partition riots of the Panjab
— are real. The stark realism of the novel, its exposition of the
human catastrophe of the partition of India, is one of its predomi-
nant qualities. Fiction is simply the form or shape the novelist has
given to documented facts and authentic events of the national past.
Every historical fact, every historical event in the novel could be
followed by a bibliographical citation. Malgonkar himself claims
authenticity in [the] "Author's Note": "only the violence in this story
happens to be true; it came in the wake of freedom, to become a part
of India's history . . . " (viii).

*A Bend in the Ganges,* then, is an impressive novel. At its best it is a story — rather a group of at least three stories — of young men's development, from the moment of their first self-awareness to that of their mature acceptance of the human condition despite the fact that Debi-dayal and Shafi Usman die before reaching the final stage of their development. Many characters, it must be said, are not developed in depth — Gandhi, Sundari, Mr. and Mrs. Tekchand Kerwad, Gopal, and others. At its worst the novel fails to cohere as a formal artistic whole. One gets the impression that there are too many episodes and too many stories which appear separate and detachable; they simply do not hang together. Furthermore, the action takes place everywhere — in a Panjab village, the Andamans, Assam, Calcutta, Lahore, Madras, and Bombay. In trying to cover everything, Malgonkar gives the impression of sketchiness and superficiality. Nevertheless, there are memorable glimpses of India in transition and enduring insights into human character that make the novel engaging, to say the least.

## CHAPTER 6

# The Novelist as Historian:
# The Devil's Wind *(1972) and*
# The Sepoy Mutiny of 1857

W HEN a literary critic comes across a book of history that he wants to condemn he will simply ask: "It is history, but is it literature?" To him an historian is a pedestrian fellow crawling laboriously through the welter and litter of documented facts. History is nothing but a bald, dry-as-dust recitation of facts. "It may be good history but it is bad prose," the critic says. To the historian, on the other hand, a novel dealing with history, appears as "pure fiction," "fairy tale," "legend." He will ask: "It is literature, but is it history?" To him a historical novelist is a strange person, a bird with wings flying away from documented facts. He says: "It may be good prose but it is bad history." These observations, I am persuaded, do not tell the whole truth about the relationship between history and fiction. In some ways history and fiction have a close kinship. The tasks of the historian and the historical novelist are, I would suggest, kindred tasks. The historian and the novelist have much in common. There are professional historians and historical novelists whose works are at once good prose and good history. There are historians whose works have literary merit — Gibbon, Macaulay, Mommsen, Churchill, and others. On the other hand there are novelists whose works reveal extensive research and careful attention to factual accuracy — Scott, Tolstoy, Mitchell, Michener, Styron, and others. Manohar Malgonkar, I am persuaded, belongs to this latter group of writers who have enlarged our understanding of the past, reducing history to a well-told tale without compromising it for the sake of the story at hand. The picture of Indian life and of India's past he constructs in *The Devil's Wind* is not inconsistent with anything historians know.

Churchill once said that he learned his history of England from Shakespeare's chronicle plays. Most of us know what little we do of major historical events, not from history books but from imaginative literature. Novels and plays often give us more enlightenment about what was happening to the world, to men and women and children, one by one, at an identifiable time and place than do statistical tables and summarizing general statements of history books. We get our knowledge of English history from the historical plays of Shakespeare; of Scottish history from the historical novels of Scott; of the Napoleonic wars from Tolstoy's *War and Peace;* of the American Civil War from Crane's *The Red Badge of Courage* and Margaret Mitchell's *Gone With the Wind;* of the Spanish Civil War from Hemingway's *For Whom the Bell Tolls;* of the Russian Revolution from Pasternak's *Dr. Zhivago;* and of the Second World War from Michener's *Tales from the South Pacific* and Hershey's *Hiroshima.* We could get our knowledge of the Sepoy Mutiny of 1857 from *The Devil's Wind.*

Certain significant moments of history or periods of national crisis have always been powerfully attractive to the novelists. Two periods of Indian history have powerfully appealed to Mr. Malgonkar's novelistic imagination. It is these two periods of tremendous stress that he dramatizes and revivifies in his novels. In the first period, 1857 - 1858, an explosion occurred which led to savage acts on both sides and brought about the end of East India Company's rule of India. The Sepoy Mutiny, as the British called it, or The First War of Independence, as the Indians called it, is the first effort by the new India to shake off British rule. The mutiny caused the British to make India a Crown Colony and to assume direct responsibility for India through the British Parliament. *The Devil's Wind* is the fictional treatment of this period. In the second period, 1938 - 1948, which was far bloodier and crueler, occurred the great Independence Movement of Gandhi, which succeeded in putting British policy and British conscience to a test. The British Labor Government decided to withdraw from India. But the advent of independence was celebrated against a backdrop of violent riots and burning villages in India and Pakistan. *The Princes* and *A Bend in the Ganges* chronicle this fatal decade of contemporary history, a decade of hope and misery, of terror and slaughter of thousands of Indians and Pakistanis. We have already taken a close look at these two novels.

These two periods offered Mr. Malgonkar the usable past for fictional treatment, the past that will help us to understand our present world in all its complexity — political, economic, social, intellectual. His primary concern is the consciousness of the past in the present. When one looks more closely at the *two* periods and the *three* novels,

one can see that Malgonkar's subject really is the wide-ranging portrait of a nation moving through time from the 1850's to the 1950's.
As Nana, the protagonist of *The Devil's Wind,* says:

"How often, during the months that followed, did we sense the nearness of
victory? And yet the pattern remained unbroken: at the last moment,
something would happen and victory would slip out of our grasp. Slowly I
began to think to myself that we were just not fated to win; that it was in pur-
suance of some divine purpose unfathomable to us that Mother India would
go on being prostituted by an alien breed; that her sons and daughters, for
some forgotten sins, would go on remaining slaves." (229)

Suppose that in some freak disaster of the future, all conventional
historical records were destroyed and only these three novels survived. How much would it be possible to learn about Indian history
from the novels? A great deal. There is evident in these novels a unique kind of imagination, the historical imagination. Malgonkar
shows man in time and place, shows him as both maker and product
of history, shows him in his full and complex historical context, and
above all, depicts him as a part of society in process. His characters,
even the imaginary characters, pass over into history as they are
usually embodiments of forces or trends in Indian history. General
Wheeler and Nana to some extent dramatize the tensions and conflicts of the times:

"I was hoping you'd tell me something about June twenty-third. No one
does."

And suddenly my heart was beating faster. I had to take a deep breath to
control my agitation. "Twenty-third of June?" I said. "What happens on the
twenty-third of June?"

"That's what I'd like to know. And remember you are speaking in the
hearing of Mother Ganges."

I laughed, almost in relief. How many lies had I not told in the hearing of
Ganga-mayi, Mother Ganges; I, a fourth-degree brahmin who had studied
all the Vedas had long ago ceased to consider myself on oath just because the
mother of rivers bore witness to what I was saying. I would have told a thousand lies rather than reveal to a British general what the twenty-third of June
1857 meant to us.

"It's the anniversary of Plassey," Wheeler prompted, "the hundredth anniversary."

Who did not know that? In our minds, the date was emblazoned in scarlet
letters that stood higher than the Himalayas. Plassey!

The period of mourning was to last for a hundred years. We knew it in our
bones. (103)

Malgonkar with his scholarly interest in history is preeminently equipped to handle these historical themes. As we have seen, his books of straight history, scholarly and exhaustive in research, deal with an important chapter of Indian history — the rise and fall of the Marathas. It is clear that Malgonkar is not only a spinner of tales but also a student of facts; he does his homework and is not too lazy to work in the library.

The essential nature of Malgonkar's historical fiction and the primary characteristics of his method can be best appreciated through a close examination of *The Devil's Wind,* a novel in which he shores up his fantasy with sturdy beams of believable and documented facts. *The Devil's Wind* is informed by a respect for history, a sure feeling for the period, and a deep and precise sense of place and time.

Like many historical novels, *The Devil's Wind* is part fact, part fiction; an historical document and a work of conscious literary art. On one level the novel presents the course of the Rebellion of 1857, especially the Rebellion in Kanpur. This is the historical narrative, or the public line of action. On another level it is the story of Nana Saheb, the young nineteenth-century prince who grows, ceases to be a spoiled prince, and emerges as one of the leaders of the revolt. This is the personal narrative or the private line of action. The two lines, public and private, are skillfully interwoven and their convergence becomes clear from a glance at Appendix 3, *Chronology of the Sepoy Mutiny,* see page 163.[1] The historical narrative, it is clear, is superimposed upon, and parallels, the personal narrative in a period of violent change. The sense of history is derived not merely from the gallery of historical figures (The Wheelers, The Hillersdons, Nana Saheb, and Tantya Topi) but from the close relationship of characters to their social and political background so that the reader feels that they could not have existed at any other moment or place of history.

Malgonkar has successfully integrated history and fiction emphasizing the relation between the course of public and private events. He attempts to give full objective description, plus subjective or emotional life of the main characters. He never fails to date happenings or mention Nana's age at the time of this or that event or to place incidents in his personal life in relation to events of national history. He skillfully scatters historical background information and explanation throughout the novel while at the same time letting Nana Saheb tell us in his autobiographical memoir a good deal about his "inward life" — his ambitions, loves, friendships, and motivations. Malgonkar has solved the problem of how much knowledge he can assume on the part of the reader and consequently how much historical information he must provide. If he provides too much, the reader will be bored; if he provides too little, he will be confused. He passes information in a manner that at the same time does not in the least prettify or falsify Nana Saheb's life that historians know. The picture of Nana's life that he constructs is not inconsistent with anything historians know.

There are, then, two stories. The first is a candid, factual narrative of the events of the Revolt of 1857 Appendix 3, *Chronology of the Sepoy Mutiny* lists these events. The second story, which underlies these events, is a fictional narrative, a kind of emotional history of the people of India, their hopes, fears, and desires; more specifically, the "inward life" of Nana Saheb, an account of what went on inside Nana, a nineteenth-century prince who in one fashion or another expresses what the revolt was all about in essence. The chronology cannot do justice to this private world of Nana. All that is done is to show Nana's private world's links with the public world — his age, his assumption of leadership, escape, etc. The first story, the story of the "National Past," is already set and cannot be tampered with. It is *the* documented history. The second story, the story of the "Personal Past," permits the novelist to engage in imaginative speculation; it allows him to speculate with a freedom not accorded to the historian — who is a slave of the documented fact, the most imperious of all historical masters — on all the intermingled miseries, ambitions, frustrations, hopes, rages, and desires of men involved in the great Revolt of 1857. It is *the* undocumented "inside" history. Malgonkar deals with the intimate undercurrent of Nana's life, the "inward life" stripping him of his external facade of personality, showing him in all his shivering moral nakedness and helplessness, in his secret world of instincts, loves, fears, and feelings. From this private world the historian is usually barred, but the novelist's chief strength lies in creating it. Nana describes his own predicament:

What happened in Meerut frightened me and made me realize that, for me, the issues were not altogether clear cut. I could not, in my own mind, separate the national struggle from personal involvements. I was on intimate terms with many British and Eurasian families; and it was well known that I had more friends among the whites than among my own kind. This was because, owing to my princely lineage, my own people tended to treat me with excessive formality; the British, with certain reservations, treated me as one of themselves. Could I now stand by and watch the men and women who had sung and danced and laughed in my house slaughtered by howling mobs? They had done no harm to me, or indeed to India. Why should they have to be sacrificed for all the wrongs piled up by the East India Company over a hundred years? (115)

## I *The Devil's Wind as history*

It will perhaps help us in understanding *The Devil's Wind* if a concise historical sketch of the Revolt of 1857 is given here. The important point is that Malgonkar does not depart from the factuality of history. As he says in the "Author's note": "This ambiguous man and his fate has always fascinated me. I discovered that the stories of Nana and the revolt have never been told from the Indian point of view. This, then, is Nana's story as I believe he might have written it himself. It is fiction; but it takes no liberties with verifiable facts or even probabilities."

*The Devil's Wind* represents the most scholarly and complex use of history. An incalculable amount of scholarly research lurks underneath its surface. Malgonkar stated in my interview with him that he spent two years on research and read over 150 books by both Britishers and Indians on this great revolt of 1857. The book bears witness to the range and depth of his historical reading, to his sharp eye for vivid or significant detail. But he lets practically nothing of this research show in the novel. This is the secret of his success. Indeed, successful historical novels are like icebergs; there is more to them than meets the eye.

The Revolt of 1857 began Sunday, May 10, 1857, when Indian soldiers called Sepoys stationed at Meerut killed their British officers, their women, and their children; marched to New Delhi, fifty miles away; captured the city without much difficulty; and proclaimed the Mughal Emperor, a helpless, bent old man of eighty-two, as their leader. The East India Company was a flaming wreck, and the British were fleeing to the fields and jungles as fugitives. The Sepoy Mutiny had begun. The rebellion swept across India from May, 1857 to July, 1858 — a period in which terrible atrocities were committed by both sides; men, women, and children, both British and Indian, were massacred. About half a million people died — about 3,000 Britishers and the rest Indians. By the end of the year the company's authority was restored, but the relations between the British and the Indians were never the same.

Delhi passed into the hands of the rebels in a few hours. Bahadur Shah was proclaimed Emperor of India against his will in his palace. A fresh crop of military risings and civil disorder swept over North India. The Mutineers received popular support in areas of Uttar Pradesh and Behar. Fortunately for the British, the mutiny spread slowly. By the end of June, 1857, Kanpur was taken by the mutineers. In *The Devil's Wind* Malgonkar turns his spotlight on the Kanpur revolt which was led by Nana Saheb. In Bundelkhand the mutineers were led by Rani of Jhansi. Delhi was recaptured by the British in September, but the rebels controlled the entire Ganges Valley.

October marked the high point of the mutineers' success. From that point on the British recaptured the rebel-held area bit by bit. In December at the Second Battle of Kanpur, the armies of the Rao Saheb and Tantia Topi were defeated by Campbell. Lucknow was recaptured in March and Jhansi fell in April. The Mutiny was substantially over by May, 1858. All the rebellions were suppressed and the British won out because the mutiny was not a concerted movement against the British.

Malgonkar's Nana Saheb is not a monster of evil as the British historians had often portrayed him to be, but a mixed up, recognizable human being like the rest of us with all the human frailties. Malgonkar does not hold him guilty of the two infamous massacres of Kanpur — Satichaura and Bibighar massacres — and he told me that he had found no evidence whatever to make Nana guilty of these crimes. This is not to say that he whitewashes history — he condemns these crimes as "monuments to Indian brutality." Recent Indian historians such as R. C. Majumdar and S. N. Sen, too, do not put the blame for these crimes on Nana Saheb. Malgonkar in this context is a positive contributor to history; he has set the record straight on these savage massacres. Nana speaks of these massacres looking at a plaque:

I was not responsible for this slaughter and had never condoned it. . . .
    A slow anger built up as I stared at my own name on the cold marble. In its sly, indirect way, it pointed an accusing finger. Even assuming that those who had murdered the women and children were my followers, was that enough reason to link my name with their crime?
    And the British knew that they were not my followers. If they had been, they would have obeyed my orders that women and children were not to be harmed. That I had given such orders was, I believe, established beyond doubt in the inquiry they had instituted after their return to Kanpur.
    It was a mean, spiteful thing to have put my name on this plaque, implying

that I was somehow at the back of it all. On the same principle, should not Queen Victoria's name be inscribed on a thousand monuments in India to suggest that she instigated the atrocities perpetrated by her subjects? . . .

It hurts because it is not true. Despite the most exhaustive inquiries, no one has been able to establish that I was anywhere near the Bibighar or even that anyone had seen me in Kanpur when the slaughter occurred, as hundreds had seen Hodson shooting the heirs of the Moghul emperor or as thousands had witnessed the public hangings of the remaining princes by Metcalfe and Boyd. (286 - 87)

Malgonkar, the historian, is preeminently a narrative rather than an analytical historian. He has not, as have many other professional historians, "repudiated the ancient allegiance of their craft to the narrative mode." Among professional historians today narrative has increasingly come to be regarded as superficial, an inadequate means of making the past intelligible. It has given way before the analytical urge. Not so with Malgonkar. In his historical novels he has successfully combined narrative and analysis in a manner in which analysis does not interrupt or violate the texture of narrative nor narrative overwhelm or drive out analysis. The marvelous and sufficient thing about history for him is that it really happened. Narrative in itself is the life blood of history. The important thing is the story, the long narrative line, and the wonder of how and what and when and who. The why, the analysis that seeks to explain, he assumes, would come out in the telling of the story. He has, of course, placed lumps of analysis in the story to help the reader understand "why," but these analytical digressions do not obstruct the flow of narrative.

He has also placed a page of quotations at the beginning, a list of the principal characters at the end, and has inserted two footnotes on pages 244 and 292, which do not interrupt the flow of narrative. In *The Devil's Wind* Malgonkar not only describes what happened but also analyzes and explains why and how. He gives us a sense of what the past felt like, what it looked like, and what emotions drove people to decisions and actions. Here is history as "heritage," hallowed with nostalgia and sustaining national pride.

## II  *The Devil's Wind* as art

The Devil's Wind is one of the best novels that Malgonkar has written, for he has got hold of a substantial theme central to the national experience — the most written about event in Indian history — and adapted it to his imaginative purposes without political or national bluster. Malgonkar had lived for a time in the former

Maratha princely state of Indore, where he first heard from his grandfather, the state's Prime Minister, of Nana Saheb, the rightful heir to the leadership of the Maratha confederacy of North India. In my interview with him he said that it was William Styron's best-selling novel *The Confessions of Nat Turner* that suggested to him not only the subject for a historical novel but also its first-person point of view.

The story is told entirely in the first person by Nana Saheb himself; the terrible events of 1857 - 58 are seen through his eyes. We are in effect being asked to spend a short lifetime in the mind and heart of this nineteenth-century prince. The author has been careful to equip his hero with a complete nineteenth-century sensibility and to expunge the twentieth century. He maintains throughout his narrative a consistent and highly imaginative realism not only on the objective plane (the politics of the dispossessed princes and landlords in 1857, the cartridges greased with pig and beef fat upsetting to Muslim and Hindu Sepoys, the cruel massacres of Satichaura, Bibighar, Kanpur, Benares, and Allahabad) but also in his imaginative recreation of the intimate psychology of his characters, the Indian rebels and their British masters. Malgonkar is here scrupulously true, true to his period, true to the nature of human beings. He remains faithful to the "feel" of what had happened, the inner dynamic, the core truth while maintaining fidelity to known facts of history.

Although little is actually known about the historical Nana — his background and early life — Malgonkar thinks of this paucity of material as an advantage to him as a novelist. He mostly invented Nana's feelings, thoughts, and experiences. No doubt Malgonkar has benefited from the perspective that historical distance of 115 years provides and the resulting ability to see the whole event clear and whole. Nana comes richly alive, both marvelously "observed" and "felt," created from a sense of withinness, from the "inner" vantage point.

Nana's thoughts and memories as he sits in Constantinople sixteen years after the event comprise a kind of interior monologue:

Once you have seen men struck down by modern weapons of war and reduced to mounds of torn, blackening flesh, horses disembowelled and fleeing in violent protest, such sights are branded with fire upon your brain. Your vision is crowded by the dead or dying. . . .

Added to these was the torment of a defeat inflicted by an enemy inferior in numbers. . . .

I thought my head would burst. In the loneliness of my room I wanted to scream at the walls and to tear down the curtains and bedclothes with my hands. Was I going mad? Shame, remorse, self-reproach were like demons taunting; I could not escape them. . . .

*Satyam-eva-jayate,* I told myself. Truth alone triumphs. We could not lose. But would even an ultimate victory — the headlong flight of the British — mitigate the torment of my mind? . . . (176 - 77)

*The Devil's Wind* can be summarized briefly. The scene is Bithoor, a small village twelve miles from Kanpur in central India to which the British had banished Baji Rao II, the Peshwa (the head of the Maratha Confederacy) after his defeat in 1818 at Poona. Nana, his adopted heir, grew up in Bithoor with no responsibilities; only limitless leisure to enjoy life and the money to buy anything he wanted. His father, whose two obsessions were sex and religion, was receiving from the British a pension of a hundred thousand pounds. The first part of the novel recaptures the splendor and the pageantry of India before 1857. Nana writes vividly of his father's sexual excesses, the beautiful women of the palace, and of his own fabulous parties and dinners given to the British. We are also told of the changing condition of India, of the discontent and unrest among large sections of the Indian population produced by the British rule. The British refusal to continue the pension to Nana after his father's death made him conspire with other discontented rulers in a vengeful revolt planned for June 23, 1857 — the centenary of the company's tyrannical rule and the day all Indians believed "The Devil's Wind would rise and unshackle Mother India." At the end of the first part of the novel Nana has reached the right age for a revolutionary — he is thirty-three years old and dispossessed. The year is 1857, the whole of North India is ablaze.

The second part deals not only with the courage and endurance of the Indians and the British but also with their demoniacal fury of hate. Mass murder was answered with massacres, hate with hate, and barbarism with barbarism. Indian and British history show nothing remotely like this. Satichaura and Bibighar, where nearly seven hundred and fifty Britishers — men, women, and children — were massacred, are monuments to Indian brutality; Allahabad, Benares, and Kanpur, where Neill and Renaud speared hundreds of Indians like hogs, are monuments to British brutality. The atrocities were not confined to one side.

The final third part, called "Gone Away," tells of the British suppression of the revolt and Nana's escape, first to Nepal, where he spends fourteen years, and then to Mecca and Constantinople, where he spends the rest of his life writing his memoir. For the British he became the "Villain of the Century," replacing Napoleon Bonaparte as the hate object. Nana was never captured by the British even though they had offered a lakh of rupees for his head.

One of the remarkable things about this novel is its accurate and convincing portrayal of mid-nineteenth-century British India. Malgonkar has a historian's eye for facts, statistics, trivia, or minutiae. He makes the dead bones of the period live by making them move. He mentioned in my interview with him that he had even checked out the weather on a particular day in 1857, whether it was rainy or cloudy, before writing about that day in *The Devil's Wind*. He makes every effort to reconstruct the feeling, the emotional and moral atmosphere, of an earlier period with the deliberate patience and care of an archaeologist. This is how Lucknow appeared to Nana:

Lucknow to me was a revelation. It was like looking at a woman raped. Admittedly, what had happened to Lucknow had happened to other places, to Allahabad and Delhi and to my ancestral Poona. But I had not seen those cities and, in any case, there it had happened long ago and the scars had been covered over with new tissue. Here I was witnessing the process of a British takeover in the raw, the deliberate and methodical tearing down of what had taken centuries to grow, and replacing it with something that had been concocted by alien minds to conform to some mercantile dream and dictated by utility. Everything that was familiar, the good and the bad, the cherished, despised, sheltered, nursed, honoured, and venerated, was dug out and left to die; old arts, crafts, old customs, an entire social structure had been hacked down. The crudest of unlettered British tradesmen were elevated above the grandees and intellectuals of Lucknow. It was not the spectacle of one rule being replaced by another so much as the uprooting of a civilization. (108)

Malgonkar's searching use of the first-person point of view and the resultant architecture of the novel merit special consideration. The general structure of the novel is intimately bound up with the first-person point of view. Like Abhay in *The Princes* Nana is the central figure in *The Devil's Wind;* not only has he played a role in the past events but he plays even a crucial role in the very act of telling of those events. He is seen both as an actor and as a narrator. Nana, the older narrator, and Nana, the younger "I" about whom he writes, evolve before our eyes during the course of the novel. We see him first as a naive and spoiled prince and later as a mature and politically conscious rebel who refuses to surrender to the British. It is through Nana's eyes that we see the Revolt of 1857, through his developing consciousness that we are made to feel the impact of those tremendous events. We get the impression of a growing, complex, and fluid personality as it is defined in the interpenetration of its past and present self-awareness:

I walked round the empty space enclosed by spiked railings where once the Bibighar had stood. Now the tablet pronounced it to have been the House of Massacre. Whether you were British or Indian, this was a shrine that could not fail to make you burn with hatred for the other race. To the British, this was a place where the women and the children held prisoners in Kanpur had been done to death only a few hours before they retook the city. . . .

To Indians, the House of Massacre will always remain a shrine to offer prayers of anger and swear oaths of vengeance, for it was a memorial as much to British atrocities as to our own. In our minds, Bibighar can never be separated from its causes or its consequences; to us, Bibighar, Fattepur, [sic] Daryaganj are interrelated, and the massacre of July 15 is only a part of its gruesome backlash. . . .

My skin prickled as I stood before this shrine to racial hatred. . . . (290)

The master stroke in the design of the novel is the self-characterization of Nana. But *The Devil's Wind* is excellent in the portrayal of other characters also — the Wheelers, the Hillersdons, Tantya Topi, and others. As a novelist Malgonkar is deeply interested in characters. Characters living in a period of momentous change presented the greatest challenge to his powers as a novelist. He was, of course, free to conjecture about private passions and motivations of both British and Indian characters. But he was careful to see that imaginative speculation was hedged about by close historical scholarship. He recreated Nana Saheb, General Wheeler, Tantya Topi, Todd, the Hillersdons, and others with the aid of historical imagination, vivid, and yet controlled by study and research. Under his pen the black and white picture of some British historians dissolves, and saints and sinners regain some measure of humanity. This is especially true of Nana Saheb, who was often portrayed as a monster of evil by the British writers. In *The Devil's Wind* he is simply a pampered prince. He is presented neither as a villainous monster nor as the forerunner of Gandhi and Nehru who brought freedom to India less than a century later. In Malgonkar's view, then, the Revolt of 1857 was more than The Sepoy Mutiny but less than The First War of Indian Independence.

This is the most profound fictional treatment of the rebellion of 1857 from an Indian point of view. *(The Nightrunners of Bengal* by John Masters presents the British view of the rebellion and its massacres.)* It is all there, put down word for word, pain for pain, agony for agony, with the precision of a surgeon and the exactitude of a mathematician and with the deep understanding of human behavior of a skilled and experienced novelist credited with other achievements to attest his qualifications. The novel could also be viewed as an historical monograph (one involuntarily looks for the footnotes). "This is the way it probably was," one says to oneself, "this is the way the great rebellion appeared to one of its leaders, this is the way it appeared to the anvil, not to the hammer."

See Appendix 3, *Chronology of the Sepoy Mutiny,* for a list of events discussed in this chapter.

## CHAPTER 7

# The Achievement of Malgonkar

A NY estimation of Malgonkar's literary worth at this time must be tentative and blurred. For this reason, one can, with a sense of novelty, still make a commonplace point. It is this: no true evaluation of an author can occur while he is still alive. At this point, Malgonkar is still productive. Moreover, there are two unpublished novels with his publishers. Speculation on the future of a productive novelist is always hazardous. All that one can do is to provide a critical progress report based primarily on what the author has produced so far — in Malgonkar's case, five published novels, three books of history, and a cluster of stories, reviews, and articles. What contribution has he made to the fiction of the twentieth century and how worthwhile is the contribution?

Malgonkar's literary career began thirteen years ago with *Distant Drum* (1960). This first novel is in content and form the least interesting and successful of his novels, though, as I have shown, it exhibits a good deal of promise. The four novels that followed this novel, however, show an increasingly tighter command of content and form. He achieves maturity — thematically and stylistically — in *The Princes* (1963), only three years after *Distant Drum*. *The Devil's Wind* (1972), his last published work to date, is a successful blend of the imagination of the historian and the imagination of the novelist. History is not presented evangelistically nor is it lacking in scholarly underpinning. No doubt it is the interaction of public and private lives that interests him. All the historical figures are in the right places, on the right dates, doing what they actually did, though conversations are mostly made up. Yet for all this documentary authenticity, how alive and immediate everything seems!

Literature may be infinite, but there is no doubt that writers repeat themselves. They have their obsessions and tricks; they learn what they can do well and what they should leave alone; they discover their strengths and weaknesses, their forte, their faults; they learn what works in their invented worlds and what does not. Such repetitions do not always imply a flagging imagination or diminution of power but rather a growing understanding. A good writer's later works remind us somewhat of his earlier ones. This is simply because he has cast aside what is unnecessary and has refined what is essential. He has learned to cultivate his own garden intensely. For a careful and serious critic there are no surprises in the later Henry James, or the later Dickens. Hardy's Wessex novels do not change but only become more Wessex; his later novels add to our knowledge of Wessex. Faulkner's Yoknapatawpha novels become more Yoknapatawpha; his later novels add to our knowledge of Yoknapatawpha. And readers of R. K. Narayan's novels have come to expect his new novels to become more Malgudi.

And so it is with the later Malgonkar. It seems strange to divide a literary career of twelve years into "earlier" and "later," but Malgonkar will be sixty-one next year; he is more than ten years older since his first novel. To take note of his age is to remind ourselves not only of his steady growth as a novelist during a brief period but also of the fact that a new Malgonkar novel is necessarily an addition to an already familiar world of imagination. We will, therefore, read it with a sense of recognition. His two unpublished novels, at present with his publishers, will continue the historical direction that we have come to expect of his novels. They will be in the familiar mainstream of his work. The action of one, as he has stated in my interview with him, is set in the period between the partition of the Indian subcontinent (1947) and the liberation of Goa (1961). And the other novel deals with the situation of a landowning politician.

The problem, as always, with Malgonkar has been the adaptation of a storytelling skill to historical subjects. When it works, as in *The Princes* and *The Devil's Wind,* the result is moving. But when story and history don't blend, as in *Distant Drum* or *A Bend in the Ganges,* then the novel droops. Malgonkar's new novel is likely to extend and clarify our understanding of his imagined world, not only the world of this particular book but the whole canon. The later work is always a further explanation of the earlier work, a new survey of old territories.

This is perhaps not the place to discuss in detail the relationship between Malgonkar's reactionary politics and the ideologicial content of his works, but we need to recognize that his works of history and fiction are peculiarly suited to convey his ultraconservative politics and reactionary ideas. There is much in his works that gives the impression of a sentimental elegy for a lost world, for the glory that was princely India. It is not surprising that he is one of the founding members of Swatantra Party, an ultraconservative political party in India. To say this is not to say that bad politics makes bad literature but to point up the fact that in the depths of his works, whether works of history or fiction, he is giving literary expression to a vague nostalgia for the vanished splendors of the past, and a passive acceptance of the *status quo* in India. He defends the kings and princes, and exhibits excessive admiration for the way of life of the ruling class in India. His Anglophilia in *Distant Drum* is part of this admiration for the ruling class or its ideology. *The Puars of Dewas Senior* and *Chhatrapatis Kolhapur* were not only commissioned by the present heads of the family of Puars and Chhatrapatis but also dedicated to them. *Chhatrapatis of Kolhapur* is dedicated "to His Highness Chhatrapati Shahaji Maharaj who has guided my steps through many an uncharted minefield of history." Critical and objective interpretation of the history of Puars and Chhatrapatis is hardly encouraged by this situation. He who pays the piper often calls the tune. Perhaps this is one of the reasons why Malgonkar's works sometimes appear to be songs of praise of a "Paradise Lost" or, to put it simply, works of propaganda for the princes. To say that they are works of propaganda is not to condemn their value. It should not be forgotten that there are many literary works which are propagandistic. Virgil wrote the *Aeneid* to glorify Roman Imperialism. Dante pamphleteered for Henry of Luxemburg. Even Shakespeare wrote patriotic propaganda in his historical plays. Propaganda by itself tells us nothing whatever about the goodness or badness of a work.

Another critical point has to be made cautiously. It is this: a writer's theories of economics and politics, no matter how well reasoned and sober, have a way of turning out to be a mere defense of his social position and financial interests. Malgonkar's works demonstrate the Marxist point that there is a correlation between a writer's class and his vision of life. Malgonkar has always been financially well-off with a comfortable and independent income from his ancestral family land to support his career as a writer. This economic fact explains the class character of his works. He is often inhibited by ideas, attitudes, values, and assumptions of his own property-owning, wealthy middle class. He cleaves to this class in his works and does not feel called upon to present the experience of another class. Nine times out of ten he chooses his principal characters from his own class. He rarely steps outside his class for his literary or historical material. There are no workers or peasants in his works; there are only princes, landlords, officers, and bureacrats. It is this class character of his works that gives the impression of a partial account of life in India. Malgonkar is more concerned with the vanities of a small upper class than with the cries in the streets of a larger lower class. There is a delicate skirting of the common life of India. He does not deal with the social and political realities of India but only with the social and political thinking of a small property-owning conservative class in India. There is no room in his works for a progressive social vision. He holds fast to the privileges of his class and his creative powers are in the service of that class. At his best and at his worst he sympathizes with the ruling class, whether British or Indian.

To say that Malgonkar's works embody the ideology of the ruling class is not to degrade his stature as a writer. Social content by itself is not helpful in the task of distinguishing the better from the worse. You cannot say that a work is first-rate simply because of its social content. Content does not exist apart from the form nor form without significant content. Form and content form a unity. Balanced criticism should take into consideration the double importance of the aesthetic and social values of a literary work. Form resides in content. To put it another way, form exists to facilitate content.

Eventually it is the art of Malgonkar, the formal qualities of his art, that we must deal with and not his politics or his class. The outstanding formal quality of his fiction is his lucid, understated, and controlled style. It is the mirror-clear style that gives his fiction its freshness, resonance, and individuality. Almost any page illustrates the ease, fluidity, lucidity, verbal economy, and control of the style, but the following two passages, one from *The Princes* about Abhay's first sight of Minnie Bradley, and the other, from *The Devil's Wind* about the monsoon in Nepal, are quite typical:

For some reason, I cannot explain, I could not drag my eyes away from the girl, for she was by no means beautiful. She sat awkwardly on her pony as though afraid of slipping off any minute, gripping the sides with her thighs and legs and yet showing a lot of light under her knees. Her face was flushed, her nose was shining and her hair was disarrayed. But I could feel that she was somehow a part of the morning, of the verve and vitality of spring, volatile and blooming, and.she was slim as a bamboo and fresh as the morning dew. As the sunlight glanced off her corn-gold hair, I went on looking at her, her femininity and helplessness a challenge to my youth. I stared until she happened to turn her face and look straight into my eyes. (131 - 32)

The Terais have been likened to a slice of paradise from October to April; they are just as surely a segment of hell during the months of monsoon. The ground becomes a bog alive with frogs and leeches and the air is thick with insects exuding sharp, medicinal smells. For four months the millions of frogs bellow ceaselessly and a vapour envelops the land, creating mysterious shapes all around you like shadows upon smoke. I would swear that the birds and all the other animals except one migrate or are suddenly struck dumb. The exception is the rhinoceros, a nightmarish creature, an amalgam of a turtle, an elephant, and a hog. This armour-plated, congenitally blind monster waddles and sleeps and noisily mates in the ooze. Everything — clothes, shoes, furniture, the barks of trees, and the walls of houses — acquires a coating of green slime, and to the rattle of the incessant rain and the booming chorus of frogs, death in the form of Terai fever comes searching you out, riding, as the Nepalese insist, not on a buffalo but on a rhino.
The Terai fever has a terrifyingly precise, unalterable cycle. A man goes down with shivers, which, the next day, give place to a raging fever. On the third day he goes into a coma. On the fifth he dies. (268 - 69)

It seems a fairly ordinary sort of prose, but on a second reading we may note certain striking stylistic features in the diction, punctuation, and syntax. Both verbally and syntactically it is possible to detect in these passages beneath the surface differences in texture some fundamental stylistic constants. First, it is clear that Malgonkar is not an innovator in language; there are no experiments in diction and syntax. His language for the most part approximates to standard British and American English in vocabulary and syntax. Occasionally, however, he uses expressions and idioms that are drawn from Indian languages. He uses, for example, the Marathi idiom "Woman with a white foot," in *The Princes,* which means "a woman who brings bad luck." Second, he prefers the specific to the general, the concrete to the abstract. Observe the references to thighs, legs, knees, face, nose, and hair in his description of an actual girl, and consider his references to the birds and animals, smells and sounds in his description of an actual monsoon. His prose is made vivid by these definite details and concrete words. Third, there is a great reliance on commas. My count of all commas would give a total of eight commas in six sentences in the first passage and nineteen commas in ten sentences in the second. Fourth, this relative frequency of commas is associated with his more pronounced tendency toward using short and simple sentences rather than long and complex or compound sentences. He prefers to use commas rather than periods, semicolons, colons, connectives, and clauses. His sentences are as simple as his vocabulary. They create the sense of a mind in the process of thinking, a mind thinking discursively, adding to, qualifying, or making more vivid some initial statement or observation. Connectives are rare in Malgonkar's prose. You are, therefore, forced to jump, rather than glide, from one stop to another. There are not many writers around in India today writing in English as their second language who can put together words or sentences as craftily as Malgonkar.

Sooner or later criticism of authors writing in English outside Britain and the United States must deal with the question: "Why in English? Can an Indian ever write good fiction in English, his second language?" Indian fiction in English needs no defending at this point in time. Mulk Raj Anand's *Untouchable* and R. K. Narayan's *Swami and Friends* appeared in 1935; Raja Rao's *Kanthapara* was published in 1938. Since the 1930's a significant body of writing in English by authors from Africa, Australia, New Zealand, the Caribbean, Canada, and India has come into existence. We should not forget, moreover, that two outstanding modern English novelists chose to write in English rather than in their mother tongues — Joseph Conrad, a Pole by birth, and Vladimir Nabakov, a Russian by birth. There is no doubt that writing in English is going on in many countries of the world alongside literary activity in their own native languages. There are nearly sixty different nations, colonies, and territories in the world where English is either the principal language or is spoken widely — a fact that has given English an unparalleled place among the world's languages. Malgonkar is in the front rank of the writers writing in English outside the monolingual empire of English, the United States and Britain. These writers have adopted their second language, English, as their medium of creative writing and introduced into English literature new continents. Chinua Achebe has introduced Africa; V. S. Naipaul has introduced the Caribbean; and Malgonkar, R. K. Narayan, Raja Rao, Mulk Raj Anand, Khushwant Singh, and others have deployed the resources of English to embody Indian experience. Malgonkar has given India an authentic voice in the international creative enterprise of using English outside Britain and the United States.

These facts concerning English writers in and outside the United

States and Britain suggest an important question: should these non-native English writers be judged by a different set of criteria than those used to judge writers writing in their own native languages? I think there should be no double standard in literary criticism. General critical standards of fiction should apply whether a writer lives in the United States or India. In this respect Malgonkar is no different from other writers in other places and times. The important question is whether or not he is successful in using English sensitively and competently as a precision instrument to explore and express an Indian vision of reality and experience. Sometimes he succeeds as in *The Princes;* at other times he fails, as for the most part in *Distant Drum* and *A Bend in the Ganges.* But fiction of an Indian, however different in vocabulary, content and form, must in the end meet the same requirements and standards as the fiction of an American or an Englishman or an African — the requirements of all fiction. Conrad, Nabakov, and Malgonkar, the bilinguals, are judged by the same standards as Hemingway and E. M. Forster, the native speakers of English. As Hemingway put it:

No writer worth a damn is a national writer or writer of the frontier or a writer of the Renaissance or a Brazilian writer. Any writer worth a damn is just a writer. That is the hard league to play in. The ball is standard, the ball parks vary somewhat, but they are all good. There are no bad bounces. Alibis don't count. Go out and do your stuff. You can't do it? Then don't take refuge in the fact that you are a local boy or a rummy, or pant to crawl back into somebody's womb. . . . You can do it or you can't do it in that league I am speaking of.

Five novels, written even in an alien language, appear to be a small achievement for a writer to claim the status of a major novelist. Nevertheless, judged by appropriate standards, Malgonkar has added to the canon of literature in English. His ability to use the English language with subtlety and sensitivity, his storytelling skill, his deeply particularizing quality of imagination, and his capacity to embody Indian experience and sensibility make his talent a rare and significant sort, if not a major talent in the twentieth century. Malgonkar is not, in any sense, a major novelist of the twentieth century like Joyce or Conrad or Hemingway. He cannot be placed in this class of supremely great novelists. Nevertheless, when one looks at all the writers writing in English outside the Anglo-American literary tradition — V.S. Naipaul, Patrick White, Chinua Achebe, and others — there is no doubt Malgonkar is one of the most rewarding minor writers in a class below that of the great masters. When one considers, on the other hand, Indian novelists writing in English — R. K. Narayan, M. R. Anand, Raja Rao, and others — one will likely agree that Malgonkar is one of the best novelists to come out of India.

I do not agree with G. S. Amur who wrote a monograph on Malgonkar.[1] He is too hesitant, tentative, and uncertain in his critical assessment of Malgonkar — he is not sure whether his works will survive. Malgonkar's place as a minor writer in international English writing outside Anglo-American monolingual literary tradition is assured. He is a major English voice in India. In his novels we pause at the depths of a young man's experiences of initiation. And through his eyes we look deep into the Indian past and begin to appreciate where we've been and to determine where we are. We can also participate in the hunt for a rogue elephant or a tiger. Malgonkar's distinctive characteristics are his strong sense of history, and of the tension between the individual and the historical forces of the time, and his capacity for seeing a human situation in close relation to its material setting. These characteristics invite comparison in some ways with other writers who have presented India in their fiction — E. M. Forster, John Masters, and Paul Scott come to mind. His fiction is Indian in the deepest sense; it shows Indians experiencing Indian culture free of fake profundity and mysticism. Not to read Malgonkar is to cheat yourself of a writer of considerable charm and skill.

# *Appendix 1*

1718 Treaty of Colaba between Kanhoji Angrey and Balaji Vishwanath. East India Company's attack on Gheria. Balaji Vishwanath's expedition to Delhi.

1720 Accession of Baji Rao Peshwa (1720 - 1740).

1721 Treaty between East India Company and the Portuguese. Anglo-Portuguese attack on Colaba.

1722 Peace Treaty between Kanhoji and the Portuguese. Dutch attack on Gheria.

1725 November 30, treaty between Shahu of Satara and Sambhaji of Kolhapur.

1726 The Battle of Sarangpur between Tukoji Puar and Girdhar Bahadur.

1728 Kanhoji Captures *Derby*.

1729 Death of Kanhoji Angrey.

1731 Kingdom of Dewas founded by Tukoji Puar.

1731 April 13, treaty of Varna between Shahu of Satara and Sambhaji of Kolhapur.

1739 Marathas capture the Portuguese Fort at Bassein. Peshwa Baji Rao founds the Maratha Empire by annexing a large part of North India.

1749 Death of Shahu.

1751 Clive's defense of Arcot.

1754 Battle of Merta between Rajput Bijay Singh and Tukoji Puar. Death of Tukoji Puar. Krishnaji Puar I succeeds.

1761 Third Battle of Panipat. Accession of Madhava Rao Peshwa I (1761 - 1772).

1762 (3) Shivaji II (1726 - 1813).

1771 Marathas capture Delhi.

1775 Raghunath Rao and the English sign a treaty.

1775- First Anglo-Maratha War.
1782

1781 Poona Court decision on the Puars.

1788 Kolhapur Kingdom shifts capital from Panhala to Kolhapur.

1789 Death of Krishnaji Puar.

1802 Treaty of Bassein between East India Company and Baji Rao.

1803- Second Anglo-Maratha War.
1805

1803 Battle of Assaye.

1813- (4) Sambhaji II (1813-1821).
1821

1817- Last Anglo-Maratha War.
1819

1818 Two branches of Puars sign a treaty of friendship with East India Company.

1821- (5) Shahaji I (1821-1838).
1838

1838- (6) Shivaji III (1838-1866).
1866

1840- Twin states of Dewas came into being.
1845
1853 Ex-Peshwa Baji Rao II dies. His adopted son Nana Saheb receives no pension.
1857 The Sepoy Mutiny. Nana Saheb in Kanpur battle.
1886 Dewas City divided.
1866- (7) Rajaram I (1866-1870).
1870
1871- (8) Shivaji IV (1871-1883).
1883
1884- (9) Shahu (1884 - 1922).
1922
1888 Birth of Sir Tukoji Rao III, Ruler of Dewas Senior.
1889 Sarangpur divided.
1899 Tukoji Rao becomes the ruler of Dewas Senior.
1907 Sir Michael Darling as Tutor to Sir Tukoji Rao III.
1908 Sir Tukoji Rao marries daughter of the Maharajah of Kolhapur.
1910 April 4, Vikramsinharao Puar born.
1912- E. M. Forster in Dewas Senior.
1913
1921 Second visit of E. M. Forster to Dewas Senior.
1922- (10) Rajaram II (1922-1940).
1940
1926 Vikramsinharao marries.
1927 Vikramsinharao leaves Dewas to stay in Kolhapur.
1937 Tukoji III dies in Pondicherry; Vikramsinharao becomes Maharaja of Dewas Senior.
1940 (11) Shivaji V (1940-1946).
1940 New Divisions of Dewas Senior and Junior.
1947 March 31, (12) Shahaji II (1947-    ). Vikramsinharao of Puar family becomes the ruler of Kolhapur as His Highness Chhatrapati Shahaji Maharaj.
1947 April, Krishraji Rao III becomes ruler of Dewas Senior.
1947 August 15, India's Independence Day.
1948 June 27, Dewas Senior merges in Madhya Bharat.
1949 March 1, Kolhapur merges in Bombay State.
1956 November 1, Madhya Bharat becomes part of Madhya Pradesh State of India.

# *Appendix 2*

N.B. Page numbers in parentheses refer to *The Princes* (P) and *A Bend in the Ganges* (B.G.).

| | |
|---|---|
| 1857 - 58 | Indian Mutiny (P. 108). |
| 1858 | East India Company's rule in India replaced by the British Crown. Queen Victoria's Proclamation (P. 11, 223). |
| 1919 | Jalianwala Bagh Massacre (B.G. 68). Three hundred seventeen Indians killed by Gen. Dyer (B.G. 253). |
| 1930 | March 12, Gandhi's Anti-Salt Campaign (P. 66, 69) to Break the Salt Law (B.G. 34). |
| 1931 | His Highness Hiroji's hatred of Nationalists (P. 71). |
| 1936 | Accession and Abdication of Edward VIII (B.G. 253). |
| 1937 | January, Elections held for Provincial Assemblies. |
| 1937 | July, Congress Ministries are formed in Bihar, Orissa, C.P., U.P., Bombay, and Madras. |
| 1938 | Status of Princely States (P. 13, 109). |
| 1939 | II World War (B.G. 127). Dewan C.P.R. Iyer's Conflict with Congress (P. 126). |
| 1939 | March, The Viceroy inaugurates The Chamber of Princes. |
| 1939 | October, All Congress Ministries Resign. |
| 1940 | August 7, "The August Offer"; The Viceroy makes a statement on India's Constitutional development. |
| 1940 | World War II (P. 129, 198). |
| 1942 | February, Fall of Singapore (B.G. 190). |
| 1942 | March, Sir S. Cripps Mission sent by Churchill (P. 222, 224; B.G. 283). |
| 1942 | April, Evacuation of Burma (B.G. 191, 253 - 54). |
| 1942 | August, Quit India (B.G. 270 - 71, 256). |
| 1944 | March, the Japanese Advance into Assam assisted by the Indian National Army of Bose (B.G. 206). |
| 1944 | Nawab of Bhopal elected Chancellor of The Chamber of Princes. |
| 1944 | The Bombay Explosion (B.G. 270). |
| 1945 | July 26, Labor Government under Attlee comes into power in Britain. |

1945    August 6, Atomic Bomb on Hiroshima (B.G. 274).

1946    January 15, Lord Wavell addresses The Chamber of Princes (P. 244; B.G. 283).

1946    May 12 - 16, Insecurity of Princes (P. 248). Cabinet Mission's statement about princely states: "Paramountcy can neither be retained by the British Crown nor transferred to the new government."

1947    January 29, Resolution of The Chamber of Princes: "Every state shall continue to retain its sovereignty and all rights and powers except those that have been expressly delegated by it. . . ."

1947    February 20, Attlee announces in Parliament the British intention of leaving India by June, 1948. Mountbatten to succeed Wavell as Viceroy.

1947    April 9, British residents in Indian States confer in Delhi.

1947    June 2 - 3, The plan for the partition of India accepted by Congress, Sikhs, and Muslim League. The plan laid down the policy of lapse of Paramountcy.

1947    July 5, New States Department inaugurated by V. Patel with a statement. Nawab of Bhopal resigns Chancellorship of The Chamber of Princes.

1947    July 18, The Indian Independence Act receives Royal Assent.

1947    July 25, Lord Mountbatten addresses the historic meeting of The Chamber of Princes (P. 264 - 66) "Tea Party with the Walrus and the Carpenter" — Nawab of Bhopal refuses to attend the meeting.

1947    July 25 - August 15, Most States sign the Instrument of Accession (P. 267 - 69; B.G. 320, 342, 349).

1947    August 15, Indian Independence Day (P. 264 - 69; B.G. 307, 349).

1947    August 16, Lord Mountbatten hands the Radcliffe Award to leaders.

1947    August 17, Radcliffe Award published.

1947    August - September, Communal disturbances, Partition riots (B.G. 319, 320, 343, 332, 344, 345).

1948    January, The Integration of States (P. 296 - 98).

1948    February 25, Merger of the State of Begwad (P. 309 - 11).

1948    April 22, Covenant signed by the rulers of the Central Indian States to form a Union called Madhya Bharat Union.

1958    November 1, Epilogue (P. 346).

# *Appendix 3*

NB. Page numbers in parentheses refer to *The Devil's Wind.*

1857   January, Rumour of "greased cartridges" started in Dum Dum (97).

1857   March, Nana 33 years old (105).

1857   May 10, Mutiny and massacre at Meerut (114).

1857   May 14, News of Meerut reaches Kanpur (112).

1857   May, Meerut Mutiny followed by outbreaks in Delhi, Ferozepur, Bombay, Bareilley, and other places.

1857   May 22, Nana entrusted by the British to take care of the treasury (199, 125 - 27). Disarming of Sepoys in Lahore, Agra, Lucknow, and Marden.

1857   June, Mutinies at Allahabad, Lucknow, Benares. Throughout June the revolt spreads through the Ganges plain. The British population in the entrenchment of Kanpur (125 - 27).

1857   June 4, Mutiny at Kanpur, and siege of European survivors (147).

1857   June 5, Nana joins the mutinous forces who returned from Kalyanpur.

1857   June 6, Nana assumes leadership of troops (148).

1857   June 23, Day of Centenary of the Battle of Plassey, when Lord Clive's victory had begun British rule (60, 169 - 74).

1857   June 26, Nana's letter addressed "To the Subjects of her most Gracious Majesty Queen Victoria."

1857   June 27, Surrender of Europeans. Satichaura Ghat Massacre of Europeans (184 - 89, 288).

1857   June 30, Ceremony to install Nana as Peshwa (194). News of Kanpur reaches Havelock at Allahabad.

1857   July 12, The first battle at Kanpur (202).

1857   July 16, Bibighar Massacre of Europeans (206 - 07, 286).

1857   July 17, Havelock enters Kanpur at the head of a victorious army advancing from Allahabad and defeats Nana (205).

1857   July 18, Nana evacuates Bithoor under cover at night.

1857   July 20, Neill arrives at Kanpur and is left in charge of Kanpur with an avenging British force. Mutinies at Indore, Agra, Mhow, and other places.

1857  August, Mutinies at Kolhapur, Jubbulpore and other places.
1857  September 14 - 20, Delhi assaulted and recaptured by the British (232).
1857  September 25, Lucknow relieved by Havelock and Outram.
1857  October, Mutiny at Bhogalpur.
1857  November, 17, Lucknow relieved by Campbell.
1857  December 6, Decisive battle of Kanpur; armies of the Rao Sahib and Tantya Topi routed by Campbell (235).
1858  January, Campbell's campaign to recapture Lucknow.
1858  March 21, Lucknow recaptured.
1858  April 3, Jhansi stormed.
1858  April 6, Final capture of Jhansi.
1858  May 27, Tantya Topi and Rani of Jhansi at gates of Gwalior (250).
1858  June 3, Rani of Jhansi and Tantya Topi proclaim the rebirth of Maratha Confederacy (250).
1858  June 6, Tantya Topi and Rani of Jhansi seize Gwalior by surprise.
1858  November 1, Queen's Proclamation (253).
1859  January, Nana escapes to Nepal (254).
1859  April 18, Tantya Topi executed (268).

# Notes and References

## Chapter One

1. All quotations in this chapter are from my two interviews with Malgonkar, unless otherwise stated: "An Interview with Manohar Malgonkar," *Lock Haven Review* no. 14 (1973), 78 - 102. (Lock Haven, Pa.) and *World Literature Written in English* vol. 12, no. 2 (Nov., 1973), 260 - 88. "The Art of Writing — An Interview with Manohar Malgonkar," *The Journal of South Asian Literature* to be published.

2. Manohar Malgonkar, "Purdah and Caste-Marks," *The Times Literary Supplement,* June 4, 1964, p. 491.

3. *Ibid.*

4. "Interview with Manohar Malgonkar." An unpublished interview by Dr. Marlene Fisher.

5. *Ibid.*

6. *Ibid.*

7. *The Times Literary Supplement* June 4, 1964, p. 491.

8. *Ibid.*

9. *The Autobiography of an Unknown Indian* (Berkeley: University of California Press, 1968), p. V.

10. "Interview with Manohar Malgonkar" by Dr. Marlene Fisher.

11. *Ibid.*

## Chapter Two

1. George Orwell, *A Collection of Essays* (New York: Doubleday, 1954), pp. 158 - 59.

## Chapter Three

1. This quotation, as others in the first chapter, is taken from my "Interview with Manohar Malgonkar."

2. *The Hill of Devi*, pp. 55 - 56.

## Chapter Four

1. The following details and the Appendix are based on: M. Edwardes, *The Last Years of British India.* London: Cassell, 1963. H. V. Hodson, *The Great Divide.* Atheneum, New York, 1971. G. D. Khosla, *Stern Reckoning.* New Delhi, 1949. E. W. R. Lumby, *The Transfer of Power in India 1945 - 47.* London, 1954. R. C. Majumdar, H. C. Raychandhuri, and K. Datta, *An Advanced History of India.* Macmillan, 1960. R. P. Masani, *The British in India.* Oxford, 1961. V. P. Menon, *The Transfer of Power in India.* Princeton: Princeton University Press, 1957. *Story of the Integration of the States.* New York: Oxford University Press, 1956. L. Mosley, *The Last Days of the British Raj.* London, 1962. B. N. Pandey, *The Break-up of British India.* Macmillan, 1969. C. M. Phiiips and Mary Doreen Wainwright, eds., *The Partition of India Policies and Perspectives 1935-1947.* The M.I.T. Press, 1970.

2. *Speeches and Documents on the Indian Constitution* (1921-47), vol. II. Selected by Sir M. Gwyer and A. Appadorai, (New York 1957), p. 771.

3. V. P. Menon, *The Story of the Integration of the Indian States* (Bombay, 1956), p. 104.

4. Quoted in H. V. Hodson, *The Great Divide,* (New York, 1971), pp. 373-74.

5. *The Last Days of the British Raj,* (New York, 1961), p. 172.

6. G. S. Amur, *Manohar Malgonkar,* (New York, 1973), p. 78.

7. Taken from my "Interview with Manohar Malgonkar."

8. See *The Puars of Dewas Senior,* pp. 266-81; *The Princes,* p. 21.

9. See *Chhatrapatis of Kolhapur,* pp. 594-97; *The Puars of Dewas Senior,* pp. 288-93.

10. Ihab Hassan, *Radical Innocence: Studies in the Contemporary American Novel* (Princeton, 1961), pp. 35-41.

11. E. M. Forster, *Aspects of the Novel* (New York, 1927), p. 239.

12. *Ibid.,* p. 240.

13. *Ibid.,* p. 242.

14. E. K. Brown, *Rhythm in the Novel* (Toronto, 1950), pp. 17-18.

15. *Ibid.,* p. 9.

## Chapter Five

1. Appendix 2, India Before and After Independence, page 161, is based on a number of historical works noted in Chapter Four. *The Princes* and *A Bend in the Ganges* show a historian's dedication to chronology and never depart from the "factuality" of history. "National Past'" is left as it is; "Personal Past" is invented.

## Chapter Six

1. Appendix 3, chronology of The Sepoy Mutiny, page 163, is based on the following books: C. Ball, *History of the Indian Mutiny,* 2 vols. London,

1859; M. Edwardes, *Battles of the Indian Mutiny,* 1963; G. W. Forrest, *History of Indian Mutiny,* 3 vols. Edinburgh and London, 1904-12; R. Hilton, *The Indian Mutiny.* Hollis and Carter, London, 1957; Rice T. Holmes, *History of Indian Mutiny.* London, 1859; J. Kaye, *History of Indian Mutiny,* 2 vols. London, 1889-93; R. C. Majumdar, et. al; *Sepoy Mutiny and the Revolt of 1857.* Calcutta, 1957; Col. G. B. Malleson, *History of the Indian Mutiny,* 3 vols. London, 1880; Col. G. B. Malleson, *Indian Mutiny of 1859.* London, 1906; Lt. Col. F. C. Maude, *Memories of the Mutiny: Which is incorporated the personal narration of John Walter Sherer,* 2 vols. London, 1894; A. Miles and A. Pattle, *The Indian Mutiny.* London, 1885; V. D. Savarkar, *The Indian War of Independence 1857.* London, 1909; S. N. Sen, *Eighteen Fifty Seven.* Delhi, 1957; P. Spear, *India: A Modern History.* Ann Arbor, 1961; W. J. Shephard, *A Personal Narrative of the Outbreak and Massacre at Cawnpore, during the Sepoy Revolt of 1857.* Lucknow, 1879; Capt. M. Thomson, *The Story of Cawnpore.* London, 1859; Sir G. O. Trevelyan, *Cawnpore.* London, 1899.

## Chapter Seven

1. G. S. Amur, Manohar Malgonkar (New York, 1973).

# Selected Bibliography

PRIMARY SOURCES

1. Fiction:

*Distant Drum*. Asia Publishing House, 1960.

*Combat of Shadows*. Hamish Hamilton, 1962, Indian Edition, Hind Pocket Books, 1968.

*The Princes*. New York: The Viking Press, 1963. A Macfadden Banner Book, 1968.

*A Bend in the Ganges*. New York: The Viking Press, 1964.

*The Devil's Wind*. New York: The Viking Press, 1972.

2. History:

*Kanhoji Angrey*. Asia Publishing House, Bombay, 1959.

*Puars of Dewas Senior*. Bombay: Orient Longmans, 1963.

*Chhatrapatis of Kolhapur*. Bombay: Popular Prakashan, 1971.


SECONDARY SOURCES

1. Books:

AMUR, G. S. *Manohar Malgonkar*. New York: Humanities Press, 1973. The only available monograph on Malgonkar. Mostly biographical and sketchy criticism. Very little close literary analysis or judgment.

CHAUDHURY, N. *An Autobiography of an Unknown India*. Berkeley: University of California, 1968.

DARLING, SIR MALCOLM. *Apprentice to Power India 1904-1908*. London: Hogarth Press, 1966. Brief references to Dewas Senior.

DERRETT, M. E. *The Modern Indian Novel in English: A Comparative Approach*. Brussels: Editions de l'Institut de Sociologie, Université Libre de Bruxelles, 1966. Includes numerous references to Malgonkar but no detailed analysis of Malgonkar's works.

DUFF, GRANT. *History of the Mahrattas*. 3 vols. Calcutta: R. Cambray, 1912.

EDWARDES, MICHAEL. *The Last Years of British India*. London: Cassel, 1963.

FORSTER, E. M. *Hill of Devi*. London, 1953. Deals with the kingdom of Dewas Senior and its Maharaja for whom Forster worked as private secretary. An excellent account.

GOKAK, V. K. *English in India: Its Present and Future.* Bombay: Asia Publishing House, 1964. Deals with the place of English in Indian literary and political life.

HODSON, H. V. *The Great Divide.* Atheneum, New York, 1971. Excellent study of recent Indian history.

IYENGAR, K. R. SRINIVASA. *Indian Contribution to English Literature.* Bombay, 1945. A useful introduction to the study of Indian writing in English.

————. *Indian Writing in English.* New York: Asia Publishing House, 1962. A comprehensive survey of the whole body of Indian writing in English.

KHOSLA, G. D. *Stern Reckoning: A survey of the events leading up to and following the partition of India.* New Delhi, 1949. A good report on the terrible events that followed Indian Independence.

LORD, J. *The Maharajas.* New York: Random House, 1971. A good introduction to the world of the Maharajas. The book includes a chapter on The Maharaja of Dewas Senior.

LUMBY, E. W. R. *The Transfer of Power in India 1945 - 47.* London, 1954. Gives detailed accounts of the period.

MAJUMDAR, R. C., K. DATTA. and H. C. RAYCHAUDHURI. *An Advanced History of India.* Macmillan, 1960. A standard work of history.

MENON, V. P. *The Story of the Integration of the Indian States.* New York, 1956. An authentic history of the integration of states by one who played a major role in the negotiations connected with the integration.

————. *The Transfer of Power in India.* Princeton: Princeton University Press, 1957. An important work of history.

MOON, PENDEREL. *Divide and Quit.* London: Chatto, 1961.

MORRIS, JOHN. *Eating the Indian Air.* New York: Atheneum, 1969. This book includes an interesting chapter on Malgonkar and his family.

MOSLEY, L. *The Last Days of the British Raj.* London, 1962. A valuable work by an Englishman about the British rule in India.

MUKHERJEE, MEENAKSHI. *The Twice Born Fiction.* Heinemann: New Delhi, 1971. Only brief references to Malgonkar. A good work on introduction to Indian novels in English.

NAIK, M. K., G. S. AMUR, and S. K. DESAI, *eds. Critical Essays on Indian Writing in English.* Dharwar: Karnatak University, 1968. The only valuable book of critical essays on Indian writing in English.

NAIPAUL, V. S. *An Area of Darkness.* London: Andre Deutsch, 1964. Includes an interesting section on Malgonkar's *The Princes.*

NARASIMHAIAH, C. D., *Fiction and the Reading Public in India.* Mysore, 1967.

ORWELL, GEORGE. *A Collection of Essays.* New York: Doubleday, 1954.

PANDEY, B. N. *The Break-Up of British India.* Macmillan, 1969.

PHILIPS, C. M. and MARY DOREEN WAINWRIGHT, *ed. The Partition of India Policies and Perspectives 1935-1947.* Cambridge, Mass.: M.I.T. Press, 1970. A valuable work of history.

PRESS, JOHN, ed. *Commonwealth Literature: Unity and Diversity in a Common Culture*. London: Heinemann Educational Books, 1965. An introductory book dealing with Commonwealth literature.

RANADE, M. G. *Rise of the Maratha Power*. Bombay, 1960.

SEN, S. N. *Eighteen Fifty-seven*. Delhi, 1957. Standard work commissioned by the government of India.

SPENCER, DOROTHY M. *Indian Fiction in English: An Annotated Bibliography*. Philadelphia: University of Pennsylvania Press, 1960. A good annotated bibliography of Indian works in English.

WALSH, WILLIAM. *Commonwealth Literature*. Oxford, New York, 1973. A very valuable introduction to the whole body of Commonwealth English writing. Has a brief chapter on India.

————. *A Human Idiom: Literature and Humanity*. London: Chatto and Windows, 1964. Has a brief chapter on R. K. Narayan.

2. Articles:

DAYANANDA, J. Y. "Rhythm in M. Malgonkar's *The Princes.*" *Literature East and West*, vol. XV, no. 1 (March, 1971), 55 - 73.

————. "The Initiatory Motifs in M. Malgonkar's *The Princes.*" *MAHFIL, A Quarterly of South Asian Literature*, vol. 8, nos. 2 - 3 (June-September, 1972), 223 - 35.

————. "M. Malgonkar's *The Devil's Wind.*" *Literature East and West*, vol. XV, no. 3 (March, 1973), 523 - 25.

————. "M. Malgonkar's *The Devil's Wind.*" *World Literature Written in English*, vol. II, no. 2 (November, 1972), 112 - 15.

————. "An Interview with Manohar Malgonkar." *Lock Haven Review*, no. 14 (1973), 78 - 102.

————. "The Art of Writing — An Interview with Manohar Malgonkar." *Journal of South Asian Literature*. To be published.

DERRETT, M. E. "The Indian Novel Written in English — A Mirror of India." In *Change and the Persistence of Tradition in India*. Ann Arbor, Michigan, 1971.

# Index

[ 173 ]